Pursuit of a Godly Life

Living Like Jesus Matters

Jody Burkeen

Copyright © December 2016 by **Burkeen Ministries LLC**

All rights reserved. No part of this publication may be reproduced, distributed, or transmitted in any form or by any means, without prior written permission.

Scripture quotations marked (ASV) are taken from the American Standard Version Bible. Accessed on Bible Gateway. www.BibleGateway.com.

Scripture quotations marked (ESV) are taken from The ESV® Bible (The Holy Bible, English Standard Version®) copyright © 2001 by Crossway, a publishing ministry of Good News Publishers. ESV® Text Edition: 2011. The ESV® text has been reproduced in cooperation with and by permission of Good News Publishers. Unauthorized reproduction of this publication is prohibited. Used by permission. All rights reserved.

Scripture quotations marked (HCSB) are taken from the Holman Christian Standard Bible®, Copyright © 1999, 2000, 2002, 2003, 2009 by Holman Bible Publishers. Used by permission. Holman Christian Standard Bible®, Holman CSB®, and HCSB® are federally registered trademarks of Holman Bible Publishers.

Scripture quotations marked (KJV) are taken from the King James Bible.

Scripture quotations marked (NASB) are taken from the New American Standard Bible ® (NASB), copyright © 1960, 1962, 1963, 1968, 1971, 1972, 1973, 1975, 1977, 1995 by The Lockman Foundation. Used by permission. www.Lockman.org.

Scripture quotations marked (NIV) are taken from the Holy Bible, New International Version. Copyright © 1973, 1978, 1984, 2011 by Biblica, Inc.® Used by permission. All rights reserved worldwide.

Scripture quotations marked (NKJV) are taken from the New King James Version®. Copyright © 1982 by Thomas Nelson, Inc. Used by permission. All rights reserved.

Scripture quotations marked (NLT) are taken from the Holy Bible, New Living Translation, copyright © 1996, 2004, 2007 by Tyndale House Foundation. Used by permission of Tyndale House Publishers, Inc., Carol Stream, Illinois 60188. All rights reserved.

Edited by: Sermon to Book

Pursuit of a Godly Life / Jody Burkeen
ISBN-10: 0-9839288-4-3
ISBN-13: 978-0-9839288-4-3

Dedication.

I want to thank my wife for sticking by me all these years. Nan has been amazing and watching her grow in the Lord has pushed me to try to know Him more. She is a godly woman and I am proud God sent her to me.

My children are growing in the Lord daily and it's a beautiful thing to watch. They have stuck by my side as well and I pray for great things in the Lord for their lives and future families.

I dedicate this book to my family!

FOREWARD

"Pursuit of a Godly Life- Living Like Jesus Matters by my good friend Jody Burkeen is just like Jody ... in your face and practical. This book hits you right in between the eyes with straight forward truth that can help any and every one. I challenge you to read it, apply it and then go out and live like Jesus matters."

Jeff Voth- Cavetime Ministries

www.cavetime.org

CONTENTS

Introduction 3
There's Something about 2 Peter 9
Diligence 12
Faith 31
Moral Excellence 46
Knowledge 65
Self-Control 81
Perseverance 101
Godliness 115
Brotherly Kindness 126
Love—with Sacrifice 139
Why a Godly Life? 148
Notes 151
About the Author 157
About Sermon To Book 159

INTRODUCTION

Battling "Easy Believism"

After spending the past few years preaching and teaching to different denominations, men's groups, conferences and seminars, I have come to this conclusion: the Christian church is obese! Not in a physical sense, (even though studies show it is that as well), but in a spiritual sense. And I don't mean this in a good way.

Time after time in these churches and church gatherings, I see many "Christians" who are lazy and uneducated in their spiritual fitness. We no longer, as a church, practice our Christianity. People are unfruitful in the true knowledge of the Lord Jesus Christ, and the number one reason for this is biblical illiteracy. Christians don't take time to read the Bible, period. And when you don't understand the Word of God, you're not living out the Word of God. You're living off of what the pastor is preaching to you—and it's not his responsibility to grow you in the true knowledge of the Lord Jesus Christ. It's yours.

This scares me for many reasons, but mostly because of the "easy believism" that is being taught in our churches today. This teaching, I believe will send a lot of people to hell!

First and foremost, I want to explain what Scripture says about salvation, because many who read this book will assume that "works" can get them to heaven. This is just not the case. Martin Luther once said "they should prove their faith by their good works." And in the book of James the author writes, "But someone may well say, "You have faith and I have works; show me your faith without the works, and I will show you my faith by my works" (James 2:18 NASB).

Faith in Jesus Christ as the Savior is the only way to receive salvation. The message of salvation is clear in the Bible. All of us have sinned and fallen short of God's glory (Romans 3:23) and because of our sin we deserve hell (Romans 6:23). However, because of His love for us (John 3:16), God took on the form of man and died as a perfect sin offering, taking on the punishment we truly deserve (Romans 5:8, 2 Corinthians 5:21). And through His promises, He offers us forgiveness of sins and eternal life in heaven to all who receive and believe, by grace through faith, in Jesus Christ as Savior (John 1:12, 3:16, 5:24; Acts 16:31).

So, where are you? Are you saved and born again? Salvation doesn't come from a prayer, but instead comes from having a true and life changing experience that starts with confessing one's belief in Jesus Christ while a repentant heart! Upon salvation, certain things should happen. First, a desire for the "truth of Scripture" should occur, a hunger for the "Word" if you will. I know from my own experience and the people I disciple, that when there is true salvation, there is true hunger for God's Word. Once this hunger starts becoming satisfied by reading and memorizing Scripture, your life should start looking different from the outside.

> *Therefore if anyone is in Christ, he is a new creature; the old things passed away; behold, new things have come.* — *2 Corinthians 5:17 (NASB)*

Secondly, upon this "true salvation" experience, your life should look different on the inside. Your desires should line up more with God's desires in the Scriptures, than with those of the world's. For example, let's say you come into Christianity believing that abortion was a choice, but through your time in the Word, you then realize that murder is a sin. Your belief structure should start changing the more you are involved in the Word. Or it may have an impact first with something like cussing. The deeper you get in the Word, the more you watch your language. Whatever it may be, upon "true salvation" the things you did yesterday or the things you desired yesterday, that contradict a godly lifestyle, should make you sad, hurt or sorrowful for acting that way. Those emotions are the Holy Spirit kicking your teeth in from the inside out. It's what we call conviction.

So, this book is written under the assumption you are saved, because the rest of this book will contain steps to grow your faith, strengthen your walk and challenge you to pursue holiness. But none of these things in and of themselves will save you without faith in Christ first, which begins with and continue to lead you to a repentant heart.

Now, let's go back to "easy-believism." This is a false teaching that is going around the church today. In essence, preachers and/ or disciple makers will lead someone through a prayer, sometimes called "the sinners prayer." Don't get me wrong, I am not teaching a works-based religion, but saying a prayer alone will not get you to heaven, just like "works" will not get you to heaven. The "sinner's prayer" is a great place to start, a great point of reference, but it's not salvation on its own. Look at what Jesus said, "Not everyone who says to Me, 'Lord, Lord,' will enter the kingdom of heaven, but he who does the will of My Father who is in heaven will enter. Many will say to Me on that day, 'Lord, Lord, did we not prophesy in Your name, and in Your name cast out demons, and in Your name perform many miracles?' And then I will declare to them, 'I never knew you; DEPART FROM ME, YOU WHO PRACTICE LAWLESSNESS'" (Matthew 7:21–23 NASB).

My fear, as I stated earlier, is that too many "Christians" are living under the assumption that because they said a prayer they are going to heaven; but where's the fruit? Jesus also said right before the last verse we looked at, "Beware of the false prophets, who come to you in sheep's clothing, but inwardly are ravenous wolves. You will know them by their fruits. Grapes are not gathered from thorn bushes nor figs from thistles, are they? So every good tree bears good fruit, but the bad tree bears bad fruit. A good tree cannot produce bad fruit, nor can a bad tree produce good fruit. Every tree that does not bear good fruit is cut down and thrown into the fire. So then, you will know them by their fruits" (Matthew 7:15–20 NASB).

So Jesus tells us that the evidence of salvation is fruit! We'll look more at biblical "fruit" later in the book.

What I see in the church is no serving (just busyness), no giving (just selfishness), no loving others (just self-love) and no salvations (just church goers). We are not living a godly life—and thus we are obese, spiritually lazy.

If you feel that you are saved, but yet spiritually lazy (we all are), then join me through the rest of this book. It will challenge you, convict you and motivate you to make a difference for God's kingdom.

If you feel you are not saved, then I encourage you today to make things right with God. Look at what Paul tells us: "Test yourselves to see if you are in the faith; examine yourselves! Or do you not recognize this about yourselves, that Jesus Christ is in you—unless indeed you fail the test?" (2 Corinthians 13:5 NASB).

Don't deceive yourself into thinking you are saved and don't let me talk you into doubting your salvation. I am just asking you to make sure that you know, that you know, that you are saved.

If you are not saved, believe in Jesus Christ, repent of your sins, and confess He is your Savior. Get into a good Bible-believing church and find someone to disciple you. Come along for a ride in the rest of this book. I hope to give you some foundation for your journey as a Christian.

This walk as a new Christian or as an old one who is just lazy is not easy, but it's worth the battle. As a matter of fact, your walk has eternal consequences for you and everyone you meet on the way!

Join me in this journey as we break down 2 Peter 1:5–12 and learn to make Jesus Lord of our life. I believe this will give the "lazy" Christian motivation to pursue God more passionately than they have in the past.

To this end, after reading each main chapter of the book, you'll find a set of questions for reflection and discussion. These workbook sections serve as a practical tool to help you get the most out of the book—to help you develop a fuller understanding of the biblical virtues outlined in 2 Peter 1:5–12 as you learn to apply them to your life and truly grow in Christ. Each workbook section also includes a practical action step.

I recommend you go through these sections with a pen in order to write your thoughts in the areas provided. Whether you go through the book and questions on your own, with a friend, or with a small group, it is my hope that *Pursuit of a Godly Life* edifies, inspires, and motivates you to live out your faith like it matters—like Jesus matters!

God bless,

Jody

PREFACE

There's Something about 2 Peter

Now for this very reason also, applying all diligence, in your faith supply moral excellence, and in your moral excellence, knowledge, and in your knowledge, self-control, and in your self-control, perseverance, and in your perseverance, godliness, and in your godliness, brotherly kindness, and in your brotherly kindness, love. For if these qualities are yours and are Increasing, they render you neither useless nor unfruitful in the true knowledge of our Lord Jesus Christ. For he who lacks these qualities is blind or short-sighted, having forgotten his purification from his former sins. Therefore, brethren, be all the more diligent to make certain about His calling and choosing you; for as long as you practice these things, you will never stumble; for in this way the entrance into the eternal kingdom of our Lord and Savior Jesus Christ will be abundantly supplied to you. Therefore, I will always be ready to remind you of these things, even though you already know them, and have been established in the truth which is present with you **— 2 Peter 1:5-12 (NASB)**

I hear all the time that Christians don't know what to do to develop or "grow" their faith, and they are confused about the process. So many give up, leave the faith all together, or just live a very mundane Christian life with little to no fruit. All too many times, "Christians" are experiencing a "false conversion" because they are unsure what to do after they say a prayer or they say it without understanding the changes that should follow.

In the passage above, Peter is writing to the church—to believers—and his point is that if you are claiming to be a Christian, if you are truly following Jesus Christ, there are certain things that should exist in your life. There are virtues that should be developing and strengthening at all times.

First, as I stated earlier, there should be the desire to change. The Holy Spirit will start changing you from the inside out. The apostle Paul writes, "Therefore if anyone is in Christ, he is a new creature; the old things passed away; behold, new things have come (2 Corinthians 5:17 NASB). Second, that desire should lead you to Scripture! I love what Paul told the Philippians, that they should "work out your salvation with fear and trembling; for it is God who is at work in you, both to will and to work for His good pleasure" (Philippians 2:12–13 NASB).

What Paul was saying here is that because of our salvation, we should work to obey God and His commands, with fear (obedience) and trembling (reverence). Because we do this, we want to know what God wants in and for us. The only way to find that out is through Scripture.

If you are not reading your Bible, you cannot understand what God's Word is telling you. Every day you should be waking up and reading your Bible! That is the only possible way you're going to continue to grow in the graces of the true knowledge of the Lord Jesus Christ. Then, Dan Ivy says we should be making "a concerted effort."[1] We should be applying something to our Christian walk, not just sitting and trying to soak it all in.

The more that I read 2 Peter 1:5–12, and the more I'm convinced God's going to convict me, the more that I should be walking away from the sins that are in my life and running toward God. That's what repentance is. Repentance is not waking up every day and saying, "God forgive me of the sin that I committed yesterday," but then doing the same thing the next day, the day after that. Rather, repentance is the sanctification process. It's about getting better each day. I'm better today in God's eyes than I was yesterday. It's a process; it doesn't automatically happen. but you've got to start with the Word of God. That's the diligence, or that's the effort that needs to be applied into your walk.

Let's stop being lukewarm. Revelation 3:16 the Lord says that "because you're lukewarm, and neither hot nor cold, I will spit you out of My mouth" (NASB). We've got to stop playing church, and we've got to start striving to love and love like Jesus.

So, 2 Peter gives us a great list of characteristics that Christians should possess and how to grow them. This book will walk through each of these virtues and show how, as a Christian, they should be progressively growing in you.

This book will show you what it means to pursue a godly life.

CHAPTER ONE

Diligence

> **Now for this very reason also, applying all diligence,** in your faith supply moral excellence, and in your moral excellence, knowledge, and in your knowledge, self-control, and in your self-control, perseverance, and in your perseverance, godliness, and in your godliness, brotherly kindness, and in your brotherly kindness, love. — **2 Peter 1:5–7 (NASB, emphasis added)**

Every year around December 28 I begin to think of my New Year's resolution. Mine usually involves lowing my weight or getting in shape, so I head to the local sporting goods store where I buy the latest fitness equipment.

I start with new shoes. Everyone knows that if you are going to be a runner, you need to take care of your feet and get good shoes. Then I get the new jogging suit—a jogging suit that will keep me warm in the winter and cool in the summer. I also don't want one so tight I look like the mannequin that was wearing it in the store.

Then I wait until January 1. That is the day I will be able to look back at in one year and remember the first step I took to getting back in shape. Then it arrives, so I get my gear on, and I head out the door. I'm so excited I run two miles. Wow, what an accomplishment! This is going to be the best year ever for my health.

Then the next morning comes. I can't feel my legs. My hamstrings "twang" when I walk because they are so tight. My toes feel like balloons and my pride, well, let's just say there is none since I just had my wife put on my socks because I can't bend over.

So, this is where my journey ends. It takes me a couple of days to recover and then my desire goes away. My shoes go in the closet and my jogging clothes in the drawer. By now I am hoping that somehow someone comes out with a pill with no side effects that will make me look like that picture I have in my mind. So I wait.

Can you relate? If so you know where I'm going with this. How many times have you decided you are going to read your Bible? Every day? We start fast and furious. We get the new Bible, new highlighters and a new notebook. We sit down and start at Genesis and by the time we hit Numbers and Deuteronomy we are spent, confused, and just plain tired. Then, the next thing you know, it's been months since we last picked up a Bible. Why does this happen so often? Well, Peter tells us the answer in the first verse of this set of Scriptures. It's lack of diligence.

The definition of diligence is a constant and earnest effort to accomplish what is undertaken[1]. It is constant persistence. God commands us to be diligent, to both learn what we should do and then diligently do it!

---

[1] Dictionary.com

The same reason I don't ever become a picture of perfect health, is the same reason Christians are lukewarm (Revelation 3:16) and that's because of a lack of a constant and earnest effort toward a goal.

In our "microwave" culture, we want everything now! We can't wait more than a few hours to get anything—thanks to technology like texting and Amazon Prime—and God forbid we ever have to exert any effort to get it. But with our faith, that is what has to happen. Peter says, "apply *all* diligence." In other words, we need to put forth effort in our faith. But how?

I believe that Christians can apply diligence to their faith in three ways: 1) Drawing on the Bible, 2) prayer, and 3) practicing repentance.

1. Diligently Drawing from the Bible

How sweet are Your words to my taste, sweeter than honey to my mouth! — Psalm 119:103 (NKJV)

The current biblical illiteracy rate among professing Christians is astronomical. Researchers George Gallup and Jim Castelli write, "Americans revere the Bible—but, by and large, they don't read it. And because they don't read it, they have become a nation of biblical illiterates."[2] This doesn't mean that Americans can't read their Bible; it means they *don't* read their Bibles.

A study done by the Barna Group[3] found these alarming stats:

- Fewer than half of all adults can name the four Gospels.
- Many professing Christians cannot identify more than two or three of the disciples.
- Sixty percent of Americans can't name even five of the Ten Commandments.
- Eighty-two percent of Americans believe "God helps those who help themselves" is a Bible verse.
- Twelve percent of adults believe that Joan of Arc was Noah's wife.
- A survey of graduating high school seniors revealed that over fifty percent thought that Sodom and Gomorrah were husband and wife.
- A considerable number of respondents to one poll indicated that Billy Graham preached the Sermon on the Mount.

Really? I wonder if these statistics describe you? If so, you may be biblically illiterate. As I stated earlier, it doesn't mean you can't read; it just means you don't.

Now don't get me wrong, I'm not talking about being a theologian, I am just talking about being a person who is actively reading, searching and trying your best to understand Scripture and its meaning in your life.

A biblically illiterate society affects people and their surroundings. It affects us personally. When you and I don't take part in a daily reading of the Word, we start to lose sight of what God gave us to guide us through this dark and cruel world. The Bible should be our first and most often source of encouragement and education, and it should be a spiritual road map for our lives. There is a delight that overcomes us when we spend time in the Word; it keeps us from getting sucked into the darkness of this world.

> *How blessed is the man who does not walk in the counsel of the wicked, nor stand in the path of sinners, nor sit in the seat of scoffers! But his delight is in the law of the LORD, and in His law he meditates day and night.* — **Psalm 1:1–2 (NASB)**

Spiritual Food

When I am discipling others, I tell people not to eat physically until they eat "spiritually." What does this mean? There is much imagery in the Bible that relates the Word of God to food that satisfies and drink that ends thirst. The psalmist writes that God "satisfies the thirsty and fills the hungry with good things."

The prophet Jeremiah wrote, "When your words came, I ate them; they were my joy and my heart's delight, for I bear your name, LORD God Almighty" (Jeremiah 15:16 NIV). Now, Jeremiah did not literally eat a parchment scroll! What does this mean, then?

Jeremiah wasn't saying he had taken a fork and a knife to the Word of God. Jeremiah was making a profound statement: The Word of God had *become a part of him.*

The human physical body needs food to survive. Eating makes digestion and thus assimilation of what was eaten possible. When the body operates normally, the result of eating is energy, health and strength, and thus a joy-filled life! But notice: Eating comes first. Food must be ground or crushed in a person's mouth in order to get the full taste out of it! It must mingle with saliva, and be chewed and chewed until the least possible amount is left to swallow. This food, ultimately, becomes a part of a person! James M. Gray writes,

> The man who does this has learned one of the great secrets of his physical being. He has learned how to keep well, and how to eat almost anything he likes without ill results. Keeping food in the mouth is the key to it all.[4]

Something like this is true in the spiritual realm. Usefulness and joy in a person's spiritual life depends on their spiritual health and strength. But these character traits, in turn, depend on a person's spiritual nourishment—its kind, its quantity, and its condition. The only true food for people's souls is the Word of God. Peter writes, "Desire the sincere milk of the word, that ye may grow thereby…" (1 Peter 2:2 KJV); the more Scripture you ingest, the more it becomes a part of who you are. It becomes a part of your innermost being.

Perhaps Job describes what eating God's Word really means:

> *I have not departed from the commands of his lips; I have treasured the words of his mouth more than my daily bread.*
> *— Job 23:12 (NIV)*

The Word of God is likened to milk (1 Peter 2:2), to honey (Psalm 19:10, 119:103) and to strong food or meat (Hebrew 5:12, 14). Faith—our spiritual life—is sustained by only through nourishment from the Word of God.

Varieties of Bible Intake

Proper diet from the Word can come in many forms:

Hearing the Word. As Jesus was teaching in the temple, "... all the people were hanging on to every word He said" (Luke 19:48 NASB). There are so many ways we can "hear the Word" throughout our day. We may not be able to follow Jesus through the village or ever hear his voice, but at our fingertips are millions of recorded videos, audio sermons, and songs of worship filled with the Word. While working, we can have any of these on in the background. While driving, they can feed and fuel us. By attending conferences, we grow from all that we are hearing from pastors and leaders who teach, or feed, us the Word.

Reading the Word. Being a diligent Christian requires dedication to get into the Word. "It shall be with him and he shall read it all the days of his life, that he may learn to fear the LORD his God, by carefully observing all the words of this law and these statutes…" (Deuteronomy 17:19 NASB). Now, some of you may not be early birds, but whatever a good time is, just schedule a time for you to read the Bible. Make sure you read you Bible every day! Start small. Read a chapter. Re-read that chapter and try to understand what

God is telling you. Then move on when you feel comfortable.

Studying the Word. "Now these were more noble-minded than those in Thessalonica, for they received the word with great eagerness, examining the Scriptures daily to see whether these things were so" (Acts 17:11). Paul commended the Bereans because they did not simply take what Paul said as truth, but went back to the Scriptures—the Old Testament—to see if it aligned up with what Paul was saying.

Memorizing the Word. "These words, which I am commanding you today, shall be on your heart. You shall teach them diligently to your sons and shall talk of them when you sit in your house and when you walk by the way and when you lie down and when you rise up" (Deuteronomy 6:6–7 NASB). Memorizing the Word of God is a vital step to the Word becoming a part of who you are. The memorized Word will drop down in to your heart and begin to transform you.

Meditating on the Word. "Finally, brethren, whatever is true, whatever is honorable, whatever is right, whatever is pure, whatever is lovely, whatever is of good repute, if there is any excellence and if anything worthy of praise, dwell on these things" (Philippians 4:8 NASB). Once you've memorized some Scripture, next meditate on it—think about it, contemplate it, and "marinate" on it. Biblical meditation has been likened to a cow chewing its cud! When a cow chews its cud, its mouth secretes saliva. This saliva contains a natural antacid that helps the cow to digest food better and to eat more feed, which helps her produce more milk. Cows spend upwards of eight hours a day chewing their cud!

This is where the Latin word *rūmināre* comes from, which means "to chew food over and over again." I'm sure you recognize the English word 'ruminate,' in that word which means "to turn something over and over in one's mind. This is biblical meditation. The famous Protestant reformer Martin Luther said rumination is "saying verses aloud to write them more deeply in us. We sing, whisper, mumble, or proclaim the Bible aloud to soak our souls in it, transforming our outlook and actions, in Christ."[5]

One thing to note: devotion and study are two different things. Bible devotion time involves sitting down in the quiet of the day and reading the Scriptures, and looking at, listening to and meditating on what God wants you to know from your reading. Then there is Bible study time. This is a pure in-depth study of the Scripture, with consideration taken of authorship, geology and the sociology of a certain book, chapter, or section of Scripture. It involves considering the cultural and historical context, which may change how you interpret a passage.

I suggest, as you are doing your devotion, that you keep a notebook nearby and write down things you want to research more in-depth later. Don't research while doing your devotion. If you decide to go deep in the understanding of the Bible and its form and function, Rick Warren wrote a book to develop a great study method, called *Rick Warren's Bible Study Methods: Twelve Ways You Can Unlock God's Word.*[6] I used this when I first started studying the Bible.

As you grow in the Word, the Holy Spirit will grow in you. This is an organic response that naturally happens as you start looking at and listening to God in His holy Word. Hearing it, reading it, studying it, memorizing it and meditating on it are all the ways to feed our spirit and nourish ourselves with all we need in our walk with God. It's not a short walk for the weak, but a long journey, so be fueled up in the Word in order to sustain a lifelong, diligent pursuit of God.

2. Diligently Praying Life

...pray continually... — *1 Thessalonians 5:17 (NIV)*

Another way to apply diligence to faith is by committing to strive for a consistent prayer life. Recall that diligence is "constant persistence." Paul writes in Ephesians 6:18 that we are to "pray in the Spirit on all occasions with all kinds of prayers and request" (NIV). We are to be continually praying!

Prayer is not magic; it is not something that guarantees we will get what we want. God is not a genie, granting wishes day in and day out! Prayer is actually for our benefit—through Jesus, we have relationship with God the Father, and this relationship is primarily engaged through our quiet communication with Him—as we slow down to listen to His voice and consider His will over our lives.

C.S. Lewis wrote about this discipline of prayer when saying, "The moment you wake up each morning all your wishes and hopes for the day rush at you like wild animals.

And the first job each morning consists in shoving it all back; in listening to that other voice, taking that other point of view, letting that other, larger, stronger, quieter life come flowing in."[7] This prayer priority is paramount for growth in faith.

Prayer Is Relationship

Prayer is a relationship between the Creator and His created beings. It means approaching God humbly and sincerely, confident that He will hear, and expectant that He will answer. This prayer relationship encompasses certain disciplines: confession, praise, adoration, supplication, and intercession. Let's consider them, for a moment, and how disciplined prayer time will contribute to your relationship with God.

Confession. Confession involves dealing honestly with sin. It means seeing our sin and agreeing with God that it is wrong. God promises that when people confess their sin to Him, "he is faithful and just to forgive us our sins and to cleanse us from unrighteousness" (1 John 1:9 ESV). Confession prepares a person's heart to hear from God. During prayer things often come to mind that may have grieved the heart of God; it is important to deal with those things, seek His forgiveness and trust God will remove that sin "as far as the east is from the west" (Psalm 103:12 ESV).

Praise. The book of Psalms is filled with praises to God. Psalm 18:3 says God is "worthy of praise" (NIV) and Psalm 21:13 says, "Be exalted in your strength LORD; we will sing and praise your might" (NIV).

Adoration. Praise means to worship and acknowledge God for who He is—His character, his faithfulness and His sovereignty over all things. In prayer, spending time adoring God recognizes His sovereignty and acknowledges He is Lord over all. When a person truly loves God, and reveres Him, they grow in relationship with Him.

Supplication. The Lord's Prayer perhaps best of all describes what supplication is: a fervent, personal petition of God for your needs, presenting requests before Him Keep in mind He will provide all of your needs, but it may not always be what you want or expected. Supplication is one small part of prayer, and yet it too often becomes the primary focus of prayer.

Intersession. Though we are to present our requests to God, we are to intercede for others as well. This is what Jesus modeled in John 17, right before He was to be crucified; yes, He presented his request before God that "this cup be removed," but he also prayed for His disciples and for those who would later believe in Him. We are to intercede and pray for each other, not just for all that we need!

Thanksgiving. God's Word often exhorts believers to be grateful for all of the good things God has done and provided for them. He is merciful, loves His children deeply, and nurtures and protects them. Thanksgiving naturally shifts one's heart from bitterness, regret or anger, to joy and rest. Disciplining yourself to having a grateful heart will naturally result in an inward awareness that God's presence is good and with you always.

In all of these areas of prayer, the believer's attitude is paramount. God's Word says we must not approach God with a haughty spirit, but in humility: "If my people, who are called by my name, will *humble* themselves and pray and seek my face and turn from their wicked ways, *then I will hear from heaven…*" (2 Chronicles 7:14 NIV, emphasis added). One must come before the other; humility opens the ears of God. Making time to spend in God's Word and making time to pray are two of the three important ways we can apply diligence to our faith; the third, repentance.

3. Diligently Repenting

Finally, "applying diligence to faith" might best be exhibited through the act of repentance. The word in the New Testament usually translated "repent" is the Greek word *metanoeo*, meaning, "to change your mind, to reconsider or to think differently."

All of the Old Testament prophets spoke about this concept of repentance, using a Hebrew word *tshuv*, meaning "to return, or to turn around." This Hebrew concept is where the idea of repentance is derived. In the New Testament, John the Baptist arrives on the scene to prepare for the Messiah's advent, calling people to "Repent, for the Kingdom of heaven has come near" (Matthew 3:2 NIV). And finally, Jesus Himself called people to repentance, echoing John: "Repent, for the kingdom of heaven has come near" (Matthew 4:17 NIV).

Though "repent" does mean to change your mind toward a certain sin in your life, the meaning of repentance goes much deeper than simply stopping a particular sin. Ultimately, true repentance is when someone who is not saved changes his and direction in life, turning away from sin and instead toward a relationship with God—and thus receives His way of salvation.

Practicing repentance means continually examining your conscience to identify and name specific sin as God reveals it to you, so that you can turn away from those things that may be destructive. Take the blame for your sinful condition before God; place blame on no one else for your offenses. Repentance also involves sorrow for sin, as "godly sorrow worketh repentance to salvation" (2 Corinthians 7:10 KJV). Ultimately, repentance leads to confessing sin. The sinner hides nothing, owns his sins and pours His heart out to his God.

Repentance Is Perpetual

Repentance happens more than once—in fact, it happens over and over all throughout a lifetime! Believers should repent until the moment God takes them home to heaven. It is a forever mindset—a constant hatred of that which is evil. This is why Paul says to "work out your salvation with fear and trembling for it is God who is at work in you, both to will and to work for His good pleasure" (Philippians 2:12b–13 NASB). It is in this place of repentance that God's children find healing from sin.

Stand Firm!

I press on toward the goal for the prize of the upward call of God in Christ Jesus. — **Philippians 3:14 (ESV)**

Peter was aware of how believers would need to press on in their relationship with God in order to grow. Without diligence, without putting forth constant and earnest effort in faith, growth will be stunted. However, persisting in reading and studying your Bible, prayer and repentance will keep your feet from slipping; you will find yourself standing on a firm foundation.

WORKBOOK

Chapter 1 Questions

Question: What ways of getting spiritual food from the Word do you practice? How can you grow in drawing on the Bible?

Doing studies like these and listening to speakers. I do need to spend more alone time in my Bible.

Question: What kinds of prayer do you practice? How can you grow in your prayer relationship with God?

I'm starting to write prayers down as I pray. I need to concentrate better.

Question: What does repentance mean to you? What kind of repentance is evident in your life? How exactly can you grow into a practice of continual repentance?

I am always repenting. Mostly because I'm always screwing up

Action: Apply diligence to your faith in three main ways: drawing on the Bible, praying, and practicing repentance. Get your fill of spiritual food by reading, studying, memorizing, and meditating on the Word. Remember that prayer takes many forms: confession, praise, adoration, supplication, and thanksgiving. Meanwhile, practice repentance as a continual process of accepting God's grace as you grow in godliness, not as a one-and-done expression of remorse. Stand firm in all of these habits of faith!

Chapter 1 Notes

CHAPTER TWO

Faith

Faith is to believe what we do not see, and the reward of this faith is to see what we believe. — **Augustine**

The American Academy of Family Physicians conducted a survey that revealed ninety-nine percent of physicians believe a relationship exists between faith and physical healing. More than one thousand health-care professionals met at Harvard Medical School to explore the relationship between spirituality and physical healing.

Interestingly, doctors' faith in faith was increased by another study in California. This research effort analyzed the effect of prayer on patients recovering from heart issues. A group of Christians was assigned about two hundred heart patients. These Christians prayed for the heart patients while the same number in a separate a control group did not receive prayer. Neither group knew about the prayers.

However, those that received prayer developed half the complications that the control group experienced.

A similar study by Dartmouth Medical School examined the effect of prayer on healing when patients prayed for themselves. Six months after bypass surgery the death was nine percent for the general population. However, for those who prayed for their personal healing, it was only five percent. Interestingly, not one of the deeply religious patients died during the period of the study.[9]

No one but God knows if the expression of faith in those who prayed for the patients influenced this higher statistic. However, one thing is clear: the results of the study changed the doctors' faith!

> Now for this very reason also, applying all diligence, **in your faith** supply moral excellence, and in your moral excellence, knowledge, and in your knowledge, self-control, and in your self-control, perseverance, and in your perseverance, godliness, and in your godliness, brotherly kindness, and in your brotherly kindness, love. — **2 Peter 5–7 (NASB, emphasis added)**

What Is Faith?

What exactly is faith? Merriam-Webster defines 'faith' as "strong belief or trust in someone or something," or "belief in the existence of God."[10] It can be strong religious feelings or a system of religious beliefs. Though this is a fine secular definition, the book of Hebrews gives us a very clear biblical definition: "Now faith is assurance of things hoped for, the conviction of things not seen" (Hebrews 11:1 NASB). What are the "things hoped for" and the "things not seen?" To answer that, let's look at one of the oldest members of the Bible's "Hall of Fame."

A Lesson from Abraham

Hebrews chapter 11 is often called the "Faith Hall of Fame." In this notable passage, the writer of Hebrews introduces an impressive list of heroic characters from the Old Testament. These men and women and their stories stand out to encourage and challenge our faith. One man in particular, is listed among these well-known Bible personalities: Abraham.

Abraham's name was originally Abram, which means, "The father is exalted." God called Abraham leave his family and go to a different country unfamiliar to him. Now, back then this was not as easy as renting a U-Haul and loading up the family furniture and driving up the interstate to a new town, stopping at fast-food restaurants along the way. No, this was a big ask. Abraham was ninety-nine years old, childless, and his wife Sarah was ninety. God had promised Abraham he would have children, and that through that "seed" God would bless the entire world (Genesis 12:1–7, Genesis 15:3–4). This was fulfilled through his line, through Isaac and then Jacob—all the way to the birth of Christ.

Abraham trusted God and believed God for the promise he could not see. Abraham never saw Jesus—and yet he had faith that God would be faithful:

> *By faith Abraham, when he was called, obeyed by going out to a place which he was to receive for an inheritance; and he went out, not knowing where he was going. By faith he lived as an alien in the land of promise, as in a foreign land, dwelling in tents with Isaac and Jacob, fellow heirs of the same promise; for he was looking for the city which has foundations, whose architect and builder is God. By faith even Sarah herself received ability to conceive, even beyond the proper time of life, since she considered Him faithful who had promised. Therefore there was born even of one man, and him as good as dead at that, as many descendants* AS THE STARS OF HEAVEN IN NUMBER, AND INNUMERABLE AS THE SAND WHICH IS BY THE SEASHORE. — ***Hebrews 11:8–12 (NASB)***

The things Abraham "hoped for" and the "things not seen" were God's promises that He would bring blessing to the all nations of the world through his seed Isaac. This of course was fulfilled in Christ—He is what was hoped for, and what could not yet be seen. Theologian A.W. Tozer said, "We can be in our day what the heroes of faith were in their day. But remember at the time ... they didn't know they were heroes."[11]

Abraham was saved because of his faith—not because of anything he did. Scripture says, "Abraham believed God, and it was counted to him as righteousness ... And to the one who does not work but believes in him who justifies the ungodly, his faith is counted as righteousness" (Romans 4:3, Galatians 3:6). His obedience to God's instruction revealed His faith, and this faith is what saved him—even though he would physically die centuries before Jesus was born!

Abraham's obedience reflected his faith. When God said, "Go!" Abraham went.

Do we do the same as Abraham?

> Faith and works are bound up in the same bundle. He that obeys God trusts God; and he that trusts God obeys God. He that is without faith is without works; and he that is without works is without faith. — **Charles Spurgeon**[12]

Characteristics of True Faith

> The faith of Christ offers no buttons to push for quick service. — **A.W. Tozer**[13]

True, real faith is not just a quick, spur of the moment decision. For the believer, it is a way of life. Paul wrote:

> *For this reason I too,* ***having heard of the faith in the Lord Jesus which exists among you*** *and your love for all the saints, do not cease giving thanks for you, while making mention of you in my prayers...* — ***Ephesians 1:15–16*** *(NASB, emphasis added)*

The faith Paul acknowledged he heard of continually existed. It was not a one-time faith. However, let's look back a few verses to see what happened *before* this ongoing faith.

In Him you also, after listening to the message of truth, the gospel of your salvation—having also believed... — **Ephesians 1:13 (NASB)**

In this verse, the word for "believed" is the Greek word *pisteuo*. *Pisteuo* comes from *pistis*, which means "to put your trust into somebody, or to believe in somebody." *Pistis* comes from *peitho*, which means "to so believe in that individual that you are willing to bow down and cast yourself and abandon yourself to Him and surrender to whatever He does." Do you see how those three words are all connected?

Once the Ephesians believed, having heard the gospel of the salvation and receiving it, they continued to believe. They continued to put their trust in Jesus, abandoning themselves to Him and surrendering to whatever He did. That's faith.

True faith also trusts God's motive when things aren't always peachy in life—when difficult situations arise. Though a situation, a disease, a layoff or even death might not make sense, the person with real faith keeps Christ as the object of that faith; they focus on Him. Theologian Charles Spurgeon wrote, "If we cannot believe God when circumstances seem be against us, we do not believe Him at all."[14]

Like Jeremiah, this person believes in the God who promised: "I will not turn away from them, to do them good" (Jeremiah 32:40). They are confident that "God causes all things to work together for good to those who love God, to those who are called according to His purpose" (Romans 8:28).

How to Increase Your Faith

The apostles said to the Lord, "Increase our faith!" (Luke 17:5 NASB). How does Jesus help them? He tells them, clearly, that faith comes by hearing, and hearing certain things will increase faith.

The central concern in accomplishing great things to further the kingdom of God has nothing to do with the quantity of faith, but God's sovereignty and power. Note what Jesus says next in Luke 17:6:

> *If you had faith like a mustard seed, you would say to this mulberry tree, "Be uprooted and be planted in the sea"; and it would obey you.* — **Luke 17:6 (NASB)**

When Jesus referred to the small mustard seed after being asked about increased faith, He deflected attention away from the quantity of faith to the *object* of faith—God! God moves mulberry trees out of the way, not us! As we trust in God's power to do all things, as we tap in to the source—*Jesus*—our faith will increase.

> *For it is by grace you have been saved, through faith—and this not from yourselves, it is the gift of God—not by works, so that no one can boast.* — **Ephesians 2:8-9 (NIV)**

But before we can tap into the source, we must *know* the source; and the only way to know the source is through the Word of God.

Faith Comes by Hearing

A lady was having an elegant party and wanted to serve mushrooms, but was a little uncertain about the mushrooms, so she fed some to the dog. He ate them and everything seemed all right, so the mushrooms were prepared and served. During the party the maid hurried to the hostess and said, "The dog is dead." The guests rushed to the hospital and had their stomachs pumped. After the confusion was over, the maid said, "That car sure did mess up the dog."

How often do we not hear what is really being said? Just having the ability to hear, doesn't mean we are receiving an accurate message. Luke tells us,

> He who has ears to hear, let him hear! — **Luke 8:8 (NKJV)**

Paul writes in Romans 10:16–17, that faith comes through hearing the Word of God: "For Isaiah says, 'Lord, who has believed what he has heard from us?' So faith comes from hearing, and hearing through the word of Christ" (ESV). And hearing is not always easy because sometimes we don't like what we hear. Parents of young children sometimes refer to it as "selective listening." When a mom talks about going to ice cream, the child might be quick to obey—but when she asks him to clean up his room, he doesn't respond. Did the child not hear? Of course he heard … but he chose not to listen.

Listening is an important part of hearing. Paul said, "Consequently, faith comes from hearing the message, and the message is heard through the word about Christ" (Romans 10:17 NIV). But only those people who desire wholeheartedly to follow God, who are actively listening with the intent to obey what He says, truly hear. Jesus said in Matthew 13:11-12 that "the knowledge of the secrets of the kingdom of heaven has been given to you, but not to them. *Whoever has will be given more, and they will have an abundance.* Whoever does not have, even what they have will be taken from them" (NIV, emphasis added).

Note that Jesus says, "Whoever has will be given more, and they will have an abundance..." (Matthew 11:12 NIV). Keep in mind, Jesus taught this within the context of saying, "He that hath ears, let him hear."

How much we desire to "hear" God through His Word determines if we will "hear"—if God will reveal—even more!

What We "Hear" Helps Us See

Actively listening to what God is saying through His Word requires the commitment to respond. Many times God will reveal things as previously discussed, that bring up sin that must be dealt with. This is what Paul meant when he said that God "made his light shine in our hearts to give us the light of the knowledge of God's glory displayed in the face of Christ" (2 Corinthians 4:6b NIV). The Word of God makes it possible to see what can't be seen on the surface; the living, active and powerful Word cuts to the heart of men and causes even the blind to see. When this happens, be quick to repent and allow God to cleanse your heart. Wisdom will "enter your heart," and your faith will increase.

> *For the LORD gives wisdom; from his mouth come knowledge and understanding. He holds success in store for the upright, he is a shield to those whose walk is blameless, for he guards the course of the just and protects the way of his faithful ones. Then you will understand what is right and just and fair— every good path. For wisdom will enter your heart, and knowledge will be pleasant to your soul.* — **Proverbs 2:6–10 (NIV)**

How to Live by Faith

> *And the Lord answered me: "Write the vision; make it plain on tablets, so he may run who reads it. For still the vision awaits its appointed time; it hastens to the end—it will not lie. If it seems slow, wait for it; it will surely come; it will not delay. Behold, his soul is puffed up; it is not upright within him, but the righteous shall live by his faith."* — **Habakkuk 2:2–4 (ESV)**

There is a short little book in the Old Testament called Habakkuk. Habakkuk was written near the end of the seventh century BC, some think just before the Babylonians took Judah captive. God told Habakkuk He would not ignore the continual evil occurring against Him, and that He was raising up a people—the Babylonians—to discipline Judah. Habakkuk was confused! How could this mode of punishment align with God's character?

God responded to Habakkuk by saying that he would indeed deal with the evil character of the Babylonians, but that "the righteous shall live by his faith."

In some Bibles, "righteous" is translated as "just." When Habbakuk wrote this, he chose the Hebrew word *saddiq*. The New Testament Greek scholar William Mounce suggests the word "describes those who act in such a way that their behavior accords with some standard." [15] It is an expression that is tightly connected in the Old Testament with judicial standing.

How a person lives their life reflects the character of their heart. Those who are ruled by the things of this world live their life reflecting this. However, Habakkuk says the righteous, in contrast, live by faith. God calls believers to live not according to the world but by faith in His instruction and commandments, which are intended for our good—and found only in the Bible. Though we might not understand, God says living this way reflects a heart that is righteous—in right standing before God. It is a heart that reflects His standard, which is holy and pure.

The Word of God is the means of living righteously. Through the words in the Bible—those living, active words that are the breath of Christ—God challenges beliefs and aligns us with His heart. Believers don't need increased faith, like the apostles requested Jesus to give them! They only need to exercise the faith they already have so that it will grow!

Jesus says if we ask for anything in His name, He will do it (John 14:14). Ask Him to help you live each day of your life with the hope promised in the Word of God! Because one day, you will see with your eyes the hope of what has been promised.

WORKBOOK

Chapter 2 Questions

Question: What are the characteristics of faith? In what areas do you need to grow—and how will you start?

_____
_____
_____
_____
_____
_____
_____
_____
_____

Question: When have you heard God's voice? How did you respond? How can you hear God's voice more often?

_____
_____
_____

Question: When you ask God for something, do you ask in faith—in Jesus' name? How do you know you're asking in faith and not in the flesh?

Action: Become a hero of the faith! Take a lesson from Abraham and hope for things unseen. Rekindle your desire to hear God—and then listen for His voice as you feed on His Word. Respond to His voice in turn, and confess to Him as the Spirit leads you. In all things, live by faith, and ask for all things in Jesus' name according to His Word and His Spirit.

Chapter 2 Notes

CHAPTER THREE

Moral Excellence

> As the excellence of steel is strength, and the excellence of art is beauty, so the excellence of mankind is moral character. — **A. W. Tozer**[16]

Exercising the faith we already have in Christ is crucial. It takes diligence, but Peter writes we should make every effort to cultivate these Christ-like qualities. Above everything in life, God is concerned about our character, and He will spend our lifetime developing it.

Pastor and writer Francis Chan introduced a message he taught on 2 Peter 1:5–11 by asking this incisive question: *"At what do you work the hardest?"*[17]

Most people would begin to create a list in their heads of the things they do—what they want to accomplish. It could be work related, recreation related or relationship related. Perhaps you are working hard to climb the corporate ladder. Or maybe you have set a goal to complete a marathon before you turn forty. Or, possibly it is working to raise godly, respectful children that others look at and wonder, "How did they raise such great kids?"

How many people would answer that question by saying they work hard at what they *are*—at their moral character?

Let's review our scripture focus from 2 Peter 1:5–7:

> *Now for this very reason also, applying all diligence, in your faith supply moral excellence, and in your moral excellence, knowledge, and in your knowledge, self-control, and in your self-control, perseverance, and in your perseverance, godliness, and in your godliness, brotherly kindness, and in your brotherly kindness, love.* — ***2 Peter 5–7 (NASB)***

This scripture that we are contemplating is all about reflecting the image of Christ. The apostle in no way is advising Christians place themselves under a set of legalistic rules and regulations that require effort to develop those qualities. In fact, he is doing quite the opposite. Our job is only to have faith in and rest in Christ—to humbly remain under His authority and control, and rely on Him and His Spirit to do the work. It is in this place of rest that God develops Christ's image in us.

However, Peter says that "in your faith" we are to supply moral excellence. What does this mean?

In very simple terms, Peter is saying, "Now it's your turn." God has provided everything we need in Him, and it is our responsibility to use what He has given. Recall that faith involves hearing—and doing should naturally come after hearing!

Peter says we are to apply all diligence and in our faith supply moral excellence. "Applying" is derived from a unique Greek word *pareisphero*. Broken in two, *pará* means "close-beside, or alongside." And *eisphéro* means "bring into." Together, the word packs a punch: it means, literally, "to bring deeply into." It means we are to do our very best in attempting to bring forth the Christian virtues Paul will next list. Isn't that profound? We are to "bring deeply into," to do our best, to diligently, in faith, supply moral excellence to others.

Where Do We Get Our Morals?

If there was ever a time of needing moral excellence, it is now. There is a verse describing the times of the Judges when there was no king and Israel was morally corrupt. The writer of Judges says that the people "did whatever seemed right in their own eyes" (Judges 21:25 NLT). Does this not describe the day and the hour we live in? Morality is relative; what is right for you might not be right for another, but each person sets heir own standard by personal and subjective opinion.

Take a look at some statistics that reflect the condition of our country, regarding morality. Michael Snyder, author of the books *The Beginning of the End* and *Get Prepared Now*, offers these statistics:[18]

- The United States has the highest teen pregnancy rate in the entire industrialized world.

- According to the National Center for Missing & Exploited Children, there are 747,408 registered sex offenders in the United States.
- The average high school boy spends two hours on adult websites every single week.
- In the United States today, more than half of all couples "move in together" before they get married.
- America has the highest divorce rate in the world by a good margin.
- The United States has the highest abortion rate in the western world. In a massacre that is almost unspeakable, more than fifty-six million American babies have been slaughtered in this country since *Roe v. Wade* was decided in 1973. Of those that get an abortion, forty-seven percent have had a previous abortion.

These are just a smattering of what could be pages and pages of deeply concerning statistics reflective of the moral code of America. Author and Bible teacher John MacArthur seems to agree, addressing this issue of morality in his book *Can God Bless America?*[19] MacArthur says that America wants God's blessing, but not God. He writes, "Our nation has systematically pushed Him out of the national consciousness—rejecting biblical morality, ignoring His word, and relying on the political and entertainment arenas for moral guidance." According to MacArthur, the result is a bankrupt nation—financially, morally and spiritually.

The "cure" for moral bankruptcy will never be found in man. Before we discuss to grow into moral excellence, let's look at what moral excellence is.

What Is Moral Excellence?

What did Peter mean when he exhorted believers to diligently pursue moral excellence? Simply put, moral excellence is a virtue. First, let's look at the word "moral." Merriam-Webster's Dictionary defines 'moral' as "relating to duty or obligation, or pertaining to those intentions and actions of which right and wrong, virtue and vice, are predicated, or to the rules by which such intentions and actions ought to be directed."[20] It relates specifically to the practice, manners or conduct of men and women as social beings and how they relate to each other, regarding right and wrong.

The word "excellence" in 2 Peter 1:5 is the Greek word *arête*, and it refers to the moral excellence of a person (in body or mind), or preeminence of a thing, an eminent endowment, property or quality. It is a virtue displayed to enrich other's lives, within the context of a social environment. It is never a virtue to be kept to oneself, but a quality that should be demonstrated to others.

However, we are sinful people, who without God will live life "according to the course of this world, according to the prince of the power of the air, of the spirit that is now working in the sons of disobedience" (Ephesians 2:2 NASB); we are futile in our thinking and darkened in our understanding (Ephesians 4:1–2). Isaiah the prophet says we can foolishly become "wise in [our] own eyes, and clever in our own sight" (Isaiah 5:21 NIV). We are fallen beings, driven by selfish motives.

G.K. Chesterton once said, "It is often supposed that when people stop believing in God, they believe in nothing. Alas, it is worse than that. When they stop believing in God, they believe in anything."[21] We want what we want, we think we know what is best, and we are hardwired for selfishness! Without God, our standard of right or wrong will always be what appeals to each person.

How then are we to know what true moral (and biblical) excellence looks like? As followers of Jesus, we have a moral code—set by the God of the universe. It is the Word of God, our plumb line for truth.

True biblical moral excellence according to the word *arête* that Peter used inherently exists only in God. Paul in Romans 13:1 says, "For there is no authority except from God" (ESV). God alone is morally excellent. Without God's Word as our moral code, we are like ships without a compass drifting in a vast sea, lost. Therefore, the Bible alone should be our source for discerning true morality. Otherwise, we will walk the wrong path.

The Bible says God wrote His law on our hearts (Romans 2:15). The best way to understand this is that God's law is our conscious—our standard for what is right and what is evil, or wrong. When a person puts their faith in Jesus Christ, they not only become a child of God, renewed and made in His image, but also as Paul writes, they "have the mind of Christ" (1 Corinthians 2:16 NIV). The Bible contains God's revealed moral will in His law and commandments—this is how God speaks to His people, and how they know His perfect, righteous character.

It is like a plumb line, a "compass" to discern true right from wrong. Sinful man is simply not able to decide what he believes right or wrong to be; it will always stem from selfish motives.

Josiah: Doing What's Right in God's Eyes

When I think of biblical characters who were faithful and committed to serving God, but also committed to moral excellence, I can't help but think of Josiah. Josiah, one of the greatest kings to ever rule Israel, was only eight years old when he advanced to the rank of king of Israel. The book of 2 Kings 22:2 says Josiah "did what was right in the eyes of the LORD" (NIV). Josiah was a good king, a man who followed God.

Some time later, while making repairs to the temple in Jerusalem, Hilkiah the high priest stumbled upon the Book of the Law—the first five books of Moses—that had been neglected and hidden for many years. It somehow had miraculously survived the reigns of many evil rulers preceding Josiah. King Josiah was broken, tore his clothes and begged God not to punish disobedient Israel. Josiah told his secretary:

> Go to the Temple and speak to the LORD for me and for the people and for all Judah. Inquire about the words written in this scroll that has been found. For the LORD's great anger is burning against us because our ancestors have not obeyed the words in this scroll. We have not been doing everything it says we must do. — *2 Kings 22:13 (NLT)*

Josiah knew the people of Israel were not living lives according to God's standards! He next brought the Book of the Law before the people and read it to all who could hear. Scripture says he made a covenant before God to follow Him and keep his commandments and statutes.

But here is the extraordinary part of this story! Look at God's response to Josiah:

> You were sorry and humbled yourself before the LORD when you heard what I said against this city and its people—that this land would be cursed and become desolate. You tore your clothing in despair and wept before me in repentance. And I have indeed heard you, says the LORD. So I will not send the promised disaster until after you have died and been buried in peace. You will not see the disaster I am going to bring on this city. — *2 Kings 22:19–20 (NLT)*

Josiah's brokenness before God, his humble attitude of repentance, saved Israel from being cursed (at least temporarily). Josiah's actions of obedience reveal a powerful example of repentance, spiritual leadership, and God's tender mercy! Josiah is a picture of moral excellence.

Just as the people had sunk to a low level of morality in the days of Josiah, doing whatever they wanted whenever they wanted, so have people today. Only those who continue to exhibit moral excellence will be called like Josiah to show leadership in dark times.

The question is, will you be a Josiah?

How to Grow in Moral Excellence

Notice what grabbed the heart of God in this story: Josiah's humility. During a time when everyone was doing what was right in their own eyes, Josiah challenged God's people to repent and do what was right according to what God says is morally right.

Something supernatural happens when God's people humble themselves. We become like Christ.

The bible says that we who have faith in Christ and submit our lives to Him become partakers in His divine nature, or His disposition:

> *He has given us his very great and precious promises, so that through them you may participate in the divine nature, having escaped the corruption in the world caused by evil desires. — 2 Peter 1:4 (NIV)*

The actual disposition of Christ is a part of us! And when we begin to fulfill God's purpose—when people begin to see God's divine nature in us—we are like Christ, and thus more "morally excellent."

Cleansed by Jesus' Blood

Jesus' death and resurrection have already cleansed us, so that we might be brought near to God to be vessels to serve Him:

How much more, then, will the blood of Christ, who through the eternal Spirit offered himself unblemished to God, cleanse our consciences from acts that lead to death, so that we may serve the living God! — **Hebrews 9:14 (NIV)**

That fact will never change; Christians were bought with the precious blood of Christ, sealed and saved for eternity. However, while on earth, the great challenge for the believer, once purified, is to remain "unstained by the world" (James 1:27 NASB). This world is not really our home anyway! Jesus said that He "chose you out of the world" (John 15:19 NASB) to be vessels for Him to use to further the gospel. But, the only way this happens is by furthering moral excellence, by the power of God's Spirit in us.

Paul exhorted believers, "Live clean, innocent lives as children of God, shining like bright lights in a world full of crooked and perverse people" (Philippians 2:15 NLT). He continued, telling the Philippians how to do this: "Hold firmly to the word of life…" (Philippians 2:16 NLT).

Hold Fast to the Word Clinging to the Word of God is the only way to increase moral excellence in your life. To "hold firmly to the word of life" means committing to reading, studying, and meditating on the living and active Word which reveals the character of God. Ultimately, this Word will move from your head to your heart, become a part of you, and ultimately transform your character to be more like His.

God's character was clearly described in a fascinating story in the Old Testament to a familiar character named Moses. After Moses had chiseled out two stones for God to write His commandments on (for the second time, by the way), He climbed Mount Sinai where the Lord descended in a cloud. God then called out His own name, passing in front of Moses:

> The LORD, the LORD, the compassionate and gracious God, slow to anger, abounding in love and faithfulness, maintaining love to thousands, and forgiving wickedness, rebellion and sin. Yet he does not leave the guilty unpunished; he punishes the children and their children for the sing of the parents to the third and fourth generations. — **Exodus 34:6b–7 (NIV)**

Names in ancient biblical times were more than an identifier for a person; names revealed something of the character of the person—ultimately, reflecting that person's father. At that moment, the Lord revealed to Moses (and thus reveals to us) who He is—what His character is like. God is longsuffering, forgiving, just, compassionate and gracious. He is slow to anger and abounds with lovingkindness.

What an amazing God we serve! But how does knowing about God's character improve our moral excellence?

We cannot grow to be like someone if we don't know that person personally. Have you ever thought it peculiar that the more you hang around a person, the more you start to take on their characteristics? Teenagers will take on the language and slang of their peers. A woman will laugh similar to her best friend. People will even dress like those they are around frequently.

The more we come to know Jesus, the more we learn about who He is and what His character is like, the more like Him we will become! This only happens through the Word of God—the vehicle God chose to reveal Himself to the world. The knowledge we gain from God's Word will impact our hearts, will thus convict us of sin, and spur us on to obey what we have learned. This is what Paul meant when he proclaimed to the Romans that their minds must be filled with the knowledge of God so that their hearts would be changed (Romans 12:1–2). In those verses, he commands that we not conform to the ways of the world; instead, we are to be transformed by the Word!

You will find your view on right and wrong will begin to shift away from what the world says is right and wrong, and toward what God says is right and wrong.

Hold firm to the Word of God, and allow it to transform your mind and your heart. Though it will take a lifetime, the process will radically change who you are in Christ.

How to Display Godly Morals

Recall what was talked about earlier in this chapter—that believers are to do their very best in striving to bring forth the Christian qualities Paul is teaching about, never trying to hoard them. Moral excellence is a quality that should be displayed to others.

Living with moral excellence in a world that is increasingly growing darker and more evil is not easy. Sometimes when a person comes to faith in Jesus Christ, they come fresh out of the very darkest, deepest pits of evil—and those situations and relationships don't always go away (at least not in the immediate). What if you are in an unhealthy marriage or a compromising job? What if your social circle participates in worldly activities?

It can seem impossible, but fortunately, God is Lord over the impossible! God does not require us to try and fix impossible situations but only set our hearts and affection on Him alone. He will do the miraculous. You only need not be afraid, and like Moses, to "Stand firm and see the LORD'S salvation He will provide for you today…" (Exodus 14:13 HCSB).

God's request of you is that you focus on Him and the Lord Jesus Christ, that you be guided by the Word of God which He promises will direct every one of your steps (Proverbs 3:6) and that you obey Him even when things don't make sense or are painful.

Of course, it would be wise to arrange your life and relationships the best you can to encourage holiness and reduce worldliness. This may mean backing away from hurtful, ungodly relationships, lustful activities, or people that will tempt you back into sin. This is called being "holy," or set apart for God. We will talk more about this in chapter 5.

Christians are also called to be in the world, but not become a part of it. They are called to be a light in the darkness! Sometimes they are the only representation of Jesus a person will come in contact with.

When you seek to live for Christ, being holy as He is holy and strive to reflect His goodness, righteousness, and faithfulness, others will see. Sometimes it won't be easy, but it will be good. Even if you should suffer for what is right, Peter says that "you are blessed"(1 Peter 3:14 NIV).

Consider the following verses from Scripture:

> *Let us not lose heart in doing good, for in due time we will reap if we do not grow weary.* — **Galatians 6:9 (NASB)**

> *But be doers of the word, and not hearers only, deceiving yourselves.* — **James 1:22 (ESV)**

> *Jesus answered, "If anyone loves Me, he will keep My word. My Father will love him, and We will come to him and make Our home with him."* — **John 14:23 (HCSB)**

> *Turn away from evil and do what is good; seek peace and pursue it!* — **Psalm 34:14 (HCSB)**

These few verses call believers to do good, be doers of the word and not just hearers, to love God and keep His Word, turn from evil and promote peace. When you live your life this way—with moral excellence—people will notice a difference. And the Word of God says they will be drawn to you. In actuality, it is not you they are drawn to, but Jesus Christ.

God does not just "hope" that you will be a godly example to others and reflect Him; He actually commands it: "Be imitators of me, just as I also am of Christ" (1 Corinthians 11:1 NASB). Your goal should always be to imitate Christ, that others might imitate you. Your moral choices, when they align with God's Word, make a difference.

When you choose not to lie, but instead tell the truth, you reflect the moral excellence of Christ. When you choose to love, rather than hate, you reflect the moral excellence of Christ. When you choose His way over your way, you reflect the moral excellence of Christ.

What will you choose?

WORKBOOK

Chapter 3 Questions

Question: What specific traits does moral excellence encompass? How do you know?

_____
_____
_____
_____
_____
_____
_____
_____
_____
_____
_____

Question: What do you work at the hardest? How exactly can you work harder at what you *are*—growing in moral excellence?

_____
_____
_____
_____
_____
_____
_____
_____
_____

Question: What is one thing you can do today, this week, this month, to submit to Gods way of moral excellence over your own.

_____
_____
_____
_____
_____
_____
_____

Action: Exercise the faith you already have by practicing moral excellence. Work as hard at what you *are* as you work at what you *do*. Like Josiah, get your morals from the Bible, and share your godly morals by what you do, not only by what you say. Grow in moral excellence: cleansed by Jesus' blood and holding fast to the Word. Remember always that you're in the world but not part of it.

Chapter 3 Notes

CHAPTER FOUR

Knowledge

> God doesn't ask us to increase our knowledge for the sake of knowledge. He asks us to increase our understanding so that we can grow into God-centered, loving, productive people. That's why we should want to know. — **Mart De Haan**[22]

Knowledge of What?

> And this is life eternal, that they might know thee the only true God, and Jesus Christ, whom thou hast sent. — *John 17:3 (KJV)*

There's a story about a proud young man who came to Socrates asking for knowledge. He walked up to the muscular philosopher and said, "O great Socrates, I come to you for knowledge." Socrates recognized a pompous numbskull when he saw one. He led the young man through the streets, to the sea, and chest-deep into water. Then he asked, "What do you want?"

"Knowledge, O wise Socrates," the young man replied with a smile. Socrates put his strong hands on the man's shoulders and pushed him under. Thirty seconds later Socrates let him up. "What do you want?" he asked again. "Wisdom!" the young man sputtered. Socrates shoved him under again. Thirty seconds passed, thirty-five. Forty. Socrates let him up. The man was gasping. "What do you want, young man?" Between heavy, heaving breaths the fellow wheezed, "Knowledge, O wise and wonderful—" Socrates jammed him under again. Forty seconds passed. Fifty. "What do you want?

"Air!" he screeched. "I need air!"

"When you want knowledge as you have just wanted air, then you will have knowledge.

Immediately, when I say the word 'knowledge,' you might think of acquiring information. To know something is to perceive it or be aware of it. Knowledge, typically, means learned information stored away in our minds.

If you were to ask yourself why you want to "know" what's in the Bible, why you want more biblical "knowledge," what would you say? To be able to answer people who have questions about God? To better understand the story of redemption? To not feel incompetent in religious conversations? Do you simply want to know more for the sake of knowing more?

"And in Your Moral Excellence, Knowledge"

> Now for this very reason also, applying all diligence, in your faith supply moral excellence, **and in your moral excellence, knowledge**, and in your knowledge, self-control, and in your self-control, perseverance, and in your perseverance, godliness, and in your godliness, brotherly kindness, and in your brotherly kindness, love. — *2 Peter 5–7 (NASB, emphasis added)*

On top of diligence, faith and moral excellence, Peter says we are to add knowledge. Does this mean God wants us to become brilliant scholars, storing away piles of information for some unknown but godly reason? Not at all! The knowledge Peter is speaking of does not come from intellectual or academic pursuits. The *Bible Knowledge Commentary* says the knowledge Peter is speaking of is spiritual knowledge, which comes only through the Holy Spirit and is focused on the person and Word of God.[23]

The Bible is clear that the knowledge of God is the most valuable knowledge a human being can possess. But it is also clear that simply being aware of God's existence is not sufficient; the knowledge of God must encompass the deep appreciation for and relationship with Him.

In order to best understand Peter's use of the word 'knowledge' in this passage, and what exactly he is encouraging us to know better, we need to consider what the word actually means in the culture and context it was actually used.

'Knowledge' is a word deep with spiritual meaning. It comes from a unique little Greek word, *gnosis*. *Gnosis* means "understanding, correct insight, truth properly comprehended and applied." *Gnosis* is functional ("working") knowledge gleaned from first hand (personal) experience, thus connecting theory with application. It is an experiential or application type of knowledge.

According to the apostle John, this type of knowledge is fostered best and grows most through obedience. In John 7, Jesus had been teaching His disciples at the Feast of Tabernacles, in Jerusalem. The wisdom coming from his mouth confounded the teachers of the law, the Jews, who questioned Him and where He learned such information—Jesus, they knew, was just a Galilean. He was not an educated man!

Jesus responded with the following:

> Anyone who chooses to do the will of God will find out (ginosko) whether my teaching comes from God or whether I speak on my own. — *John 7:17 (NIV)*

Jesus proclaimed that if any man was, "willing to do the will of God" he "would know" whether the teaching was of God or not. Do you see the close connection between doing—or obedience—and knowing?

There is a profound link between how we respond to God's commands in Scripture, and knowing Him more intimately. Charles Spurgeon describes this "adding" of knowledge this way: "As you have seen the mason take up first one stone, and then another, and then gradually build the house, so are you Christians to take first one virtue, and then another, and then another, and to pile up these stones of grace one upon the other until you have built a palace for the indwelling of the Holy Ghost."[24]

Knowledge is but another virtue in the building up of your spiritual dwelling place of the Lord: Christ in you, the hope of glory. As believers walk in obedience to the Word of God, they come to know God through that experience. And God wants this understanding of who He is to continue to be built "one stone of grace upon the other."

Knowledge That Increases

For the Christian, faith in Jesus is the starting point, but we are to keep going! We are to study the Bible and "grow in the grace and knowledge of our Lord and Savior Jesus Christ" (2 Peter 3:18 NIV). God intends for our knowledge of Him—the depth of our relationship and love for Him—to increase.

> For this reason, since the day we heard about you, we have not stopped praying for you. We continually ask God to fill you with the knowledge of his will through all the wisdom and understanding that the Spirit gives, so that you may live a life worthy of the Lord and please him in every way: bearing fruit in every good work, **growing in the knowledge of God**, being strengthened with all power according to his glorious might so that you may have great endurance and patience, and giving joyful thanks to the Father, who has qualified you to share in the inheritance of his holy people in the kingdom of light. — **Colossians 1:9–12 (NIV, emphasis added)**

Preacher and writer Guy King once wrote about how people get to know each other, and compared it with knowing Christ. "The acquaintance with people generally proceeds in orderly sequence," King wrote. First, there is the introduction; King compares this to when we first came to Christ. Then, King says there "is to be increase," when Jesus calls His disciples to "follow me" in Matthew 4:19 (NIV). This step of following Jesus begins the process of growth. Finally, King says the following:

> All this can lead up to intimacy—so beautifully demonstrated in Peter's case, along with his two fellow-apostles, James and John, in Jairus' house, on the Transfiguration Mount, and in the Gethsemane garden. Let us make no mistake; the Lord has no favorites, but He has intimates, who are prepared to pay the cost in absolute devotion, and complete consecration. You will recall that [in Philippians 3:10] the apostle tells us that in his pursuance of knowledge, his chief ambition was, "that I may know Him." Such close fellowship and understanding embodies "all wisdom" indeed![25]

Because knowledge is a gift from God (Proverbs 2:6), and it is His to give, those who revere God will receive it. The writer of Proverbs reminds us, "The fear of the LORD is the beginning of knowledge…" (Proverbs 1:7 NIV). The word fear does not refer to a feeling of dread or terror, but of deep reverence and respect for God. Fear of the Lord submits humbly to His instruction, His will and His authority over our life. The natural result of one who fears God is obedience! And overflowing from obedience comes knowledge.

If we try to understand God on our own, we will be like a hamster on a wheel; we will get nowhere fast. Human knowledge is flawed, and according to the Bible it is worthless for it is not tempered by love (1 Corinthians 13:2). Human knowledge tends to puff man up, contrasting with godly knowledge that is grounded in love and "builds up" (1 Corinthians 8:1 NIV). Thus, for the Christian, godly knowledge implies there must be relationship.

Notice that when Jesus was teaching His disciples about what it means to follow Him, comparing it to a sheep following their shepherd, He strategically chose to use the word 'know':

> I am the good shepherd; I **know** my sheep and my sheep know me. — ***John 10:14 (NIV, emphasis added)***

However, when speaking to the Jewish religious leaders who were trying their best to find fault in Jesus, Jesus said, "You do not *know* me or my Father…" (John 8:19 NIV, emphasis added). These Jewish religious leaders, though they knew the Scriptures inside and out—memorizing longs passages from the time they were little boys—were far from God.

Therefore, to know Christ is to have faith in Him, to follow Him, to have a relationship with Him, to love and be loved by Him.

But God does not want His children to remain in a causal relationship with Him! He wants them to grow in the knowledge, experientially, of who He is. This is what it means to mature in Christ. Consider the following verses:

> …but speaking the truth in love, we are to grow up in all aspects into Him who is the head, even Christ. — ***Ephesians 4:15 (NASB)***

> But we urge you, brethren, to excel still more… — ***1 Thessalonians 4:10b (NASB)***

> *...so that you will walk in a manner worthy of the Lord, to please Him in all respects, bearing fruit in every good work and **increasing in the knowledge of God**... — Colossians 1:10 (NASB, emphasis added)*

This growth, this "increase" in knowledge is speaking of spiritual growth. And try as we might, we simply cannot make ourselves grow on our own. Only God causes growth. Paul wrote to the Corinthians, "I planted, Apollos watered, but God was causing the growth. So then neither the one who plants nor the one who waters is anything, but God who causes the growth" (1 Corinthians 3:6–7 NASB).

How to Increase Your Knowledge of God

Clearly it is God alone who causes growth in a believer. He has not left us alone to our own means to try and figure out how to know the God who created all things! Where would we begin?

God inspired men to write down, over thousands of year, His very Word so that we would be able to study it—this living and very active Word—and grow in understanding of who God is. But this is where the believer must not be passive. There are three things the believer who wants to grow must commit to doing, out of obedience to God: Study the Scriptures, pray diligently, and fellowship with other believers.

Study the Scriptures

First, let's look at the purpose of Scripture. The purpose of the Bible is to reveal who God is—ultimately, manifested in the person of Jesus Christ.

We should not approach Scripture to know more about God, but to know God. The unbelieving Jews searched out the Scriptures for the wrong reasons; caught up in legalism, they studied and worked hard to know the rules and regulations: "You study the Scriptures diligently because you think that in them you have eternal life" (John 5:39 NIV). Jesus said. And yet, they missed the one the Scriptures spoke of: "These are the very Scriptures that testify about me" (John 5:39 NIV). Solomon described God's Word in an intimate way that implies a deep relationship with a person: "When you walk, they [God's commandments] will guide you; when you sleep, they will watch over you; when you awake, they will speak to you." Reverend Carl Haak writes, "This is because the Word of God is actually the revelation of God! The pages of the Bible, to the believing heart, are like mirrors, mirrors reflecting God in the face of Jesus Christ."[26]

Pray Diligently

Not only do we come to the knowledge of God through the study of the Scriptures, but we also can increase our knowledge of Him through the act of prayer. Prayer is simply communication with God—a way of bringing the Word of God that you have stored up in your mind and heart before Him—and listening for Him to guide you further into truth. Bible teacher Greg Herrick writes: "Our knowledge of God is absolutely crucial to our relationship with him and our prayer lives. Prayer is carried to God in faith. Faith is, in large measure, dependent on who we think God is. Therefore, the vibrancy of our prayer lives is directly dependent on our thoughts and our personal knowledge of God.

Fellowship with Others

Throughout the New Testament the theme of fellowshipping with other believers runs thick. Through Paul God encourages us to "not [give] up meeting together…" (Hebrews 10:25 NIV). Perhaps this was because God knew how important fellowship would be in increasing knowledge of Him. God reveals Himself through His Word, and intimately through prayer, but often He will affirm what He has been teaching you in His Word and in your prayer time through others. Fellowship encourages, uplifts, sharpens and comforts. Above all, Jesus promises that "where two or three are gathered in my name, there am I with them" (Matthew 18:20 NIV). When in the presence of other believers, God is present, too!

God wants so much for us to know Him intimately! He is waiting to reveal Himself to us so that we might know Him more. We have a choice to make each day—will we turn to Him and seek to know Him more than the day before?

I recall hearing an analogy of a young shepherd boy with his sheep. This shepherd loves all of his sheep and longs to express this love to each one individually. However, he is only able to show that love in a close way to those sheep that are happily frolicking beside him or lying at his feet. Those that are wandering off, climbing rocks or playing in the water are not loved any less; they just don't experience that love in the same way.

Jesus wants to reveal Himself to each one of us, to express that love that is so deep and wide, so that we might know Him. But like the shepherd boy, He can show that love to those who are keeping in step with Him, right as His feet.

Are you?

What Do I Do with This Knowledge?

> Let us occupy ourselves entirely in knowing God. The more we know Him, the more we will desire to know Him. As love increases with knowledge, the more we know God, the more we will truly love Him. We will learn to love Him equally in times of distress or in times of great joy. — **Brother Lawrence**[27]

Jesus clearly associates the obtaining of knowledge of God (*gnosis*, or experiential knowledge) with a willingness to obey God's will. This virtue involves a diligent study and pursuit of truth in the Word of God. This kind of knowledge does not come automatically but calls for obedience. It is the result of coming into a deeper relationship with God—it matures our faith, and through this maturity, we come to know Him better and pursue a life that reflects Him to others. True spiritual knowledge will not only govern, but it will change the way we live.

In Judaism, there is a simple yet profound prayer called the Shema. It is the cry of the Jewish person's heart, a statement of their faith before God. It is said or sung every day, and it derived directly from the Old Testament, from Deuteronomy 6:

> *Hear, Israel, the L*ORD *our God, the L*ORD *is One.*
>
> *Blessed be the Name of His glorious kingdom for ever and ever.*
>
> *And you shall love the Lord your God with all your heart and with all your soul and with all your might.*
>
> *And these words that I command you today shall be in your heart.*
>
> *And you shall teach them diligently to your children, and you shall speak of them*
>
> *when you sit at home, and when you walk along the way, and when you lie down and when you rise up.*
>
> *And you shall bind them as a sign on your hand, and they shall be for frontlets between your eyes.*
>
> *And you shall write them on the doorposts of your house and on your gates.*

The very first word of Deuteronomy 6:4, the first line of the Shema, is 'hear.' The Hebrew word for 'hear' is the name of the prayer, *shema*. However, *shema* means much more than listening. A child might hear his mother ask two, three, four times to put his shoes and socks on but never respond. This is not *shema*.

Shema is "listening with the intent to obey." It is active listening. Knowledge of God involves this kind of hearing. It means committing to respond to and obey to whatever God says! That might seem a bit scary, but it is through active listening that we come to know God in a way we could never have imagined! Seek God, search Him out in the Scriptures, ask to know Him in increasing measure, and then wait expectantly. Be prepared to obey whatever He might ask of you! And you might be surprised as your desire for him increases as well.

WORKBOOK

Chapter 4 Questions

Question: How do you get your knowledge of God? How badly do you want more?

_____
_____
_____
_____
_____
_____
_____
_____
_____
_____

Question: In which area—study of Scriptures, prayer, or fellowship with others—do you most need to grow? How exactly can you grow in this respect?

Question: How do you put your knowledge into practice? In what areas have you not been living out your knowledge fully in obedience—and how will you change?

Action: Desire knowledge of God and His ways as bad as you want to breathe! Increase your knowledge of God by studying the Scriptures, praying diligently, and fellowshipping with others. And once you have knowledge, live in obedience to it!

Chapter 4 Notes

CHAPTER FIVE

Self-Control

> It is impossible to be a follower of Jesus without giving diligent attention in our lives to the grace of self-control. —
> **Jerry Bridges[28]**

An interviewer asked Edmund Hilary, the first man who to ever conquer Mount Everest, about his passion for climbing mountains. Hilary gave this reply: "It is not the mountain we conquer but ourselves."

Tsar Peter the Great of Russia, who expanded Russian Tsardom into a vast empire that became the foremost European power in the 1600s, said, "I have been able to conquer an empire, but I have not been able to conquer myself."

We have a different kind of "mountain" to conquer: our self. And what a massive mountain it is! Trying to subdue the selfish, needy, lustful and prideful bodies God has given us is no small job.

King Solomon, who composed most of the book of Proverbs, seemed to have some understanding of this issue. Solomon wrote, "Like a city whose walls are broken through is a person who lacks self-control" (Proverbs 25:28).

"And in Your Knowledge, Self-Control"

> *Now for this very reason also, applying all diligence, in your faith supply moral excellence, and in your moral excellence, knowledge,* **and in your knowledge, self-control***, and in your self-control, perseverance, and in your perseverance, godliness, and in your godliness, brotherly kindness, and in your brotherly kindness, love.* **— 2 Peter 5–7 (NASB)**

It is not by chance Peter speaks of self-control immediately after commissioning believers to grow in the knowledge of God. He calls Christians to add self-control to knowledge. How is self-control related to knowledge?

As we earlier discussed, knowledge involves diligently studying the Word of God, praying, and fellowshipping with other believers. The natural response should be obedience to God. One of the key motifs throughout Scripture is obedience, so it makes sense Peter's first indication of active obedience would be controlling self-focused human tendencies. It is this response to knowledge—obedience—that links the two together. But truly, this is where the rubber meets the road. Man fights against obedience! However, obedience leads to living "deeply, thoughtfully, and in communion with God in the everyday pathways of our lives," says Gary Thomas, author of *The*

Glorious Pursuit: Embracing the Virtues of Christ. In this book, he proclaims that (the obedient life) is "the only life that brings true, lasting fulfillment and the inner satisfaction of being fulfilled."[29]

So then, to experience this type of inner satisfaction, we must learn self-control. What does self-control mean, from a biblical perspective? In the original Greek, the word for self-control is *enkrateia*, derived from the words *en kratos*, meaning "dominion, mastery, or power to rule." It means literally to hold oneself to possess the ability to take a grip of one's self. It is "the character of one who masters his desires and passions, and especially his sensual (sexual) appetite." So, self-control is the inner power to restrain personal passions, cravings, or lust.

Paul calls these inner desires "desires of the flesh":

> So I say, walk by the Spirit, and you will not gratify the desires of the flesh. For the flesh desires what is contrary to the Spirit, and the Spirit what is contrary to the flesh. They are in conflict with each other, so that you are not to do whatever you want. But if you are led by the Spirit, you are not under law. The acts of the flesh are obvious: sexual immorality, impurity and debauchery; idolatry and witchcraft; hatred, discord, jealousy, fits of rage, selfish ambition, dissensions, factions and envy; drunkenness, orgies, and the like. I warn you, as I did before, that those who live like this will not inherit the kingdom of God. — **Galatians 5:16–21 (NIV)**

Two things rule a person's life: the flesh (pride and self-will) and the Spirit (God). The flesh formulates moral weakness, and according to Richard J. Krejcir, it "includes our receptiveness and propensity to sin, our inability to see our own situation and respond in kind as God would have us do."[30] Krejcir continues by saying that we are given the Holy Spirit to be energized by God to live and work His way. The problem is, while living on this earth, we will still possess the propensity to sin. It is our natural sinful nature to desire wrong and to destroy. Paul affirms sin's power by saying, "Therefore, just as sin entered the world through one man, and death through sin, and in this way death came to all people, because all sinned" (Romans 5:12 NIV).

The path to uncontrolled life, one led by selfish motives as a result of sin, results from unchecked passions and defiance against God to walk in obedience to His instruction.

God calls us to a different standard. He calls us to fight against those sinful desires of the flesh through His grace, and the power of His Spirit. This grace "teaches us to say 'No' to ungodliness and worldly passions, and to live self-controlled, upright and godly lives in this present age..." (Titus 2:12 NIV). We must control ourselves. We must do what is right. We must lead godly lives in today's world.

By the Power of the Spirit

Even though believers are saved from eternal death and separation from God the moment they put their faith in Him, and even though they have the Spirit of Christ dwelling within them, the old flesh is still an active force they must continually contend with. Author and theologian

John Piper writes, "The very concept of "self-control" implies a battle between a divided self."[28] He continues, "It implies that our 'self' produces desires we should not satisfy but instead 'control'."[31]

It is as if God is saying, "Get a grip on yourself!"

How is a Christian to control himself? Let's start by examining one short verse in the New Testament:

> But I say, **walk** by the Spirit and you will not carry out the desires of the flesh. — *Galatians 5:16 (NASB, emphasis added)*

In Galatians 5:16, the word "walk" grammatically is written in what is called the present imperative. The present imperative means to continually or habitually follow the command given. Often, in the Bible, it is a call to a long-term commitment and calls for the attitude or action to become a person's habitual way of life—or more simply, their lifestyle.

Thus, Paul says the only way to "not carry out the desire of the flesh"—to fight sinful desires, passions, and sexual appetites—is for a person's lifestyle to continually, invariably and habitually be walking intimately with God's Spirit.

Christians already possess this gift, but they must, however, toil for it. Paul said he labored with the Spirit, "struggling with all his energy that he powerfully works within me" (Colossians 1:29 ESV). Paul also wrote that "if by the Spirit you put to death the deeds of the body you will live" (Romans 8:13 ESV). Clearly, it is only by the power of the Spirit in the believer that they may experience victory over the desires of the flesh.

Just as the Israelites were promised the land but had to take it by force, one town at a time, Piper writes that "we too are promised the gift of self-control—yet we must take it by force." It's not as simple as saying "no" to a certain sin and experiencing instant relief from temptation. Self-control is a gift from God, a fruit of the Spirit:

> But the fruit of the Spirit is love, joy, peace, patience, kindness, goodness, faithfulness, gentleness, self-control; against such things there is no law. — **Galatians 5:22–23 (NASB)**

Embrace this gift! Learn to trust quietly in God and lean into Him to fight temptations that are beyond what even the strongest Christian can win on his own. Satan is well aware of people's weaknesses and will do anything he can to try to deceive/tempt/entice? God's children to give in to sin.

A traveler in Sri Lanka told the following story: "As I was dining in a home, I was startled to hear the hostess ask her servant to place a bowl of milk on the deer skin beside her chair. I knew at once that there was a cobra in the room, for they prefer milk to anything else. We also knew that a hasty movement meant death, so we sat like statues. Soon, to our amazement, a cobra uncoiled from my hostess' ankle and swiftly glided toward the milk, where it was quickly killed." [32]

What a triumph of self-control over the external! But if we use the same quiet trust in Christ as this woman did in the bowl of milk, when the serpent of all evil approaches us, internal victories over him would be more numerous than they are now.

What Does Biblical Self-Control Look Like?

Submitting Your Bodies to God

One of the primary areas Scripture focuses on regarding mastering self-control is in the area of sexual purity. God gave man and woman the desire for each other and pleasure of sexual intimacy, but Scripture also is clear on the importance of remaining within the boundaries He set. "It is God's will that you should be sanctified: that you should avoid sexual immorality; that each of you should learn to control your own body in a way that is holy and honorable, not in passionate lust like the pagans who do not know God ... For God did not call us to be impure, but to live a holy life" (1 Thessalonians 4:3–5, 7 NIV, emphasis added).

Notice the phrase "each of you should learn to control your own body." The author of 1 Thessalonians, Paul, had just addressed sexuality and immediately commands Christians to control their bodies in that same area. When believers give in to sexual immorality, the Holy Spirit is not controlling them but rather their desires. Controlling lusts and desires is paramount for anyone who claims to know Jesus Christ. Consider Paul's words:

> *Flee immorality. Every other sin that a man commits is outside the body, but the immoral man sins against his own*

> body. Or do you not know that your body is a temple of the Holy Spirit who is in you, whom you have from God, and that you are not your own? For you have been bought with a price: therefore glorify God in your body. — **1 Corinthians 6:18–20 (NASB)**

When the Christian exerts self-control over their physical body in the area of sexual purity, it honors God.

Submitting Your Moods to God

The Bible is full of instruction on the importance of controlling our moods; yes, a person may have a bad day or sleep poorly the night before or experience hurt or betrayal—all reasons to slip into a bad mood! It may even seem justified because of the situation. However, God does not justify bad moods. Instead, He gives some very clear instruction on what to do when experiencing them:

> I know what it is to be in need, and I know what it is to have plenty. I have learned the secret of being content in any and every situation, whether well fed or hungry, whether living in plenty or in want— **Phil 4:12 NIV**

> Search me, O God, and know my heart; try me and know my anxious thoughts... — **Psalm 139:23 (NASB)**

God doesn't give freedom to wallow in anger or anxiety, but instead calls Christians to control that angry and worrisome spirit—and even indicates the person who is able to exhibit self-control over emotions is better and mightier than a city-conquering king! Invite God in and allow His Spirit to control any anxious or angry thoughts. Paul says, "The mind set on the flesh is death, but the mind set on the Spirit is life and peace," echoing a verse from the Old Testament where God Himself said, "I have set before you life and death, blessings and curses. Now choose life…" (Deuteronomy 30:19 NIV).

It is possible to conquer swinging moods—but only for those whose minds are set on the Spirit, on life and peace.

Renowned theologian R.C. Sproul said, "Anger is not in itself sinful, but … it may be the occasion for sin. The issue of self-control is the question of how we deal with anger. Violence, tantrums, bitterness, resentment, hostility, and even withdrawn silence are all sinful responses to anger."[33] Soon, those responses to anger, if not controlled, will lead to sin.

Submitting Your Tongues to God

A woman approached an old Puritan priest of London and told him that the bands that he wore with his pulpit gown were too long, and they annoyed her greatly. She asked his permission to shorten them. Confident of his permission, she had come prepared with a pair of scissors in hand. The priest complied and gave up the offending bands to the woman, who shortened them according to her taste with her scissors, returning the pieces to the minister.

He thanked her and said: "Now, my good woman, there is something about you that is too long, and which has bothered me greatly, and since one good turn deserves another, I would like permission to shorten it." The woman responded, "Certainly! You have the license to do so, and here are the scissors." The preacher said, "Very well, madam, put out your tongue."

Though just a story, this anecdote touches on a small but deadly weapon that, if not controlled, is evil and full of lethal poison: the tongue. The bible also says that the tongue defiles the entire body and sets on fire the course of a person's life! With the same tongue, a person can speak a blessing to one and lies, evil, and malice to another (James 3:6-10).

Now, it's not the actual tongue that's the problem. Scripture identifies the tongue just project the words that overflow from what is in a person's heart:

> The good man out of the good treasure of his heart brings forth what is good; and the evil man out of the evil treasure brings forth what is evil; for his mouth speaks from that which fills his heart. — *Luke 6:45 (NASB)*

No unwholesome talk should come out of our mouth! This means guarding against filthy language—cussing, gossip, or lying—that for some people might be the hardest area in life to master! This is what James meant when he exhorted believers to "tame the tongue" (James 3:8a). Again, it is only by the power of God's Spirit in the believer that a person can master these things. Profanity, obscenities, dirty jokes—each of these falls into the category of what the Bible says are "out of place" for the believer in Christ:

> Nor should there be any obscenity, foolish talk or coarse joking, which are out of place, but rather thanksgiving. — **Ephesians 5:4 (NIV)**

> ...rid yourselves of ... filthy language... — **Colossians 3:8 (NIV)**

How is the Christian to control these issues? Paul says we should speak "rather [with] thanksgiving" (Ephesians 5:4 NIV), but how do we train and tame our sinful tongues? Good news! We have help! Because the Spirit of Christ who raised Jesus from the dead is alive (and at work) in you (Romans 8:11 NIV)! Washington Irving once said, "A sharp tongue is the only edge-tool that grows sharper with constant use." Don't give the enemy the upper hand. Control a sharp tongue with the help of the Spirit, so that it never grows sharp enough to damage or hurt others or yourself.

Submitting Your Finances to God

The world tells people it's okay to go into debt to get what you want. Cheating and dishonest gain are smiled upon. Generosity with money is not common.

However, in God's economy, things work a bit backwards. It is more blessed to *give* than receive (Acts 20:35).

God also says that "where your treasure is, there your heart will be also" (Matthew 6:21 NIV). If a person's treasure is in the material things they are "storing up" on earth—houses, cars, boats, big-ticket toys—God says the heart is in tow.

Those who do not master greediness become slaves to it, and Jesus said it is impossible to serve "both God and mammon" (Matthew 6:24 ASV). "Mammon" is an ancient Aramaic word that points to wealth or material gain. Jesus is saying that when money (or the pursuit of what a person can buy with money) becomes the focus of fulfillment or happiness, this then becomes an issue of self-control. The need for money often misplaces people's trust. They begin to trust in whatever it is that provides more money—a job, a person, an inheritance or a savings account—and not in the Giver of all good things.

Paul offers the solution for the believer, explaining to his young disciple Timothy what a person's focus should be on:

> As for the rich in this present age, charge them not to be haughty, nor to set their hopes on the uncertainty of riches, but on God, who richly provides us with everything to enjoy. They are to do good, to be rich in good works, to be generous and ready to share, thus storing up treasure for themselves as a good foundation for the future, so that they may take hold of that which is truly life. — *1 Timothy 6:17–19 (ESV)*

God calls people to be obedient in this area—to have a servant's heart that is generous and ready to share with others. He calls believers to store up things in heaven, which is the true way to "invest" in the future.

He is Master of all things related to finances. None of it belongs to us anyway—we just manage it for Him. And He is calling us to be wise and self-controlled stewards of what He has so generously given. For He says, "Keep your life free from love of money, and be content with what you have, for he has said, 'I will never leave you nor forsake you'" (Hebrews 13:5 ESV).

Obeying God by being self-controlled in the area of finances results in a deeper knowledge of Him as provider and protector.

Learning to Respond like Jesus

One of the hardest areas for people to control is how they respond to hurt or betrayal. However, there is no one who better understands this than Jesus. Those closest to Him—Peter and Judas— betrayed Him. Scripture says, "He came to his own people, and even they rejected him." Jesus, a Jewish man and Savior of the world, came to the nation of Israel, and they did not believe who He was.

It is to Him we must look for how to respond when experiencing deep hurt or betrayal from anyone—but especially those closest to us:

> *For you have been called for this purpose, since Christ also suffered for you, leaving you an example for you to follow in His steps, WHO COMMITTED NO SIN, NOR WAS ANY DECEIT FOUND IN*

HIS MOUTH; **and while being reviled, He did not revile in return**; *while suffering, He uttered no threats, but kept entrusting Himself to Him who judges righteously...* — **1 Peter 2:21–23 (NASB, emphasis added)**

When hated, Jesus did not hate back. When he was suffering the most unimaginable pain as he hung dying on a cross and was taunted and humiliated before men, he said nothing. Rather than hating those who were crucifying Him, He begged the father to forgive them, "for they do not know what they are doing" (Luke 23:34 NIV). However, Jesus did do something, and the believer who wishes to remain self-controlled in their reactions to others must do the same-- Jesus kept entrusting Himself to a God who righteously judges. He trusted His Father to best to handle it

God's instruction is different than the world's. Those who are controlled by the Spirit look different; they respond unusually to injury and hate. Paul says it like this:

So, as those who have been chosen of God, holy and beloved, put on a heart of compassion, kindness, humility, gentleness and patience; bearing with one another, and forgiving each other, whoever has a complaint against anyone; just as the Lord forgave you, so also should you. Beyond all these things put on love, which is the perfect bond of unity.
— **Colossians 3:12–15 (NASB)**

The Christian who exhibits self-control responds and reacts like Jesus–with compassion, kindness, humility, gentleness and great patience. They are quick to forgive, and above all, they love well.

> We must have a spirit of power towards the enemy, a spirit of love towards men, and a spirit of self-control towards ourselves. — **Watchman Nee**[34]

Learning to Flee

Kent Crockett tells the following story in his book *The 911 Handbook*: A couple of boys tried to walk through a corral when a bull saw them and began to charge. One of the boys said, "Let's stop and pray." The other boy said, "No, let's run and pray!"[35] They didn't need to resist the bull inside of the corral. They needed to run out of the area where they were vulnerable to a safe place instead. That's what we need to do when we are being tempted. We need to flee from the temptation.

> In the same way, choosing to resist temptation while remaining in an environment of it is like trying to withstand the bull inside of the corral! Yes, God calls people to pray when experiencing temptation. Through Paul God said, "No temptation has overtaken you except what is common to mankind. And God is faithful; he will not let you be tempted beyond what you can bear. But when you are tempted, he will also provide a way out so that you can endure it" (1 Corinthians 10:13 NIV).

Remaining in the same environment surrounded by everything that sparkles and entices (what Paul calls in 1

John 2:16 the desires of the eyes that are not from the Father) is not obeying wisdom from the Father but is falling for the trickery of the enemy, and is like asking for death, rather than life.

The word resist comes from the Greek word *anthístēmi*, which means, "to take a complete stand against, or to take a contrary position against." It means refusing to be moved. However, Jennifer LeClaire writes in her article "You're Resisting the Devil, So Why Won't He Flee?" that we can't take a complete stand against an enemy with whom we are standing in some measure of agreement.[36] The book of James says:

> But he gives us more grace. That is why Scripture says: "God opposes the proud but shows favor to the humble." Submit yourselves, then, to God. Resist the devil, and he will flee from you. Come near to God and he will come near to you. Wash your hands, you sinners, and purify your hearts, you double-minded. — *James 4:6-8 (NIV)*

LeClaire writes, "When you keep this Scripture in context, then it offers a clue about why the devil may not flee: We aren't fully submitted to God." God promises to draw near to those who draw near to Him in humility. Remaining in the environment of temptation puts you right in the battlefield; Satan will always try to make sin look desirable. And though it is not sinning to be tempted (Jesus was tempted in the wilderness) it becomes sin when one gives in to the temptation. The best way to battle the possibility of sin is to avoid anything, anyone, or anywhere that will lead to temptation.

Jesus warned that the spirit is indeed willing, but often the flesh is too weak to withstand the temptation. Therefore, as John Dryden says, "Better [to] shun the bait, than struggle in the snare."[37]

Resist the devil and he will flee from you. But first, get out of the corral! That bull will hurt!

WORKBOOK

Chapter 5 Questions

Question: What areas in your life do you most struggle with self-control even though you know better? What exactly will you do to change?

_____
_____
_____
_____
_____
_____
_____

Question: What are the areas in your life from which you need to run and pray instead of standing and praying?

_____
_____
_____
_____
_____
_____
_____

Question: On the whole, does the Spirit or the flesh moreso rule your life? What can you do to cooperate with the changes God may want to make in you?

Action: In your knowledge of God's Word, practice self-control. Let the Spirit, not the flesh, rule you! Living in obedience, by the power of the Spirit, will lead to a God-controlled life. But although you have the gift of the Spirit, you still have to make a constant effort to walk with Him. For instance, maintain sexual purity, turn your moods over to God, cut out ungodly speech, and manage your finances in a godly way—generously, responsibly, and with a servant's heart. When you're hurt or betrayed, don't lash out; instead, respond with compassion and forgiveness. And don't hesitate to flee from temptation—it's strength, not cowardice, to "run and pray." Make God your lifestyle choice by putting your knowledge to work and exercising self-control! action challenge?

Chapter 5 Notes

CHAPTER SIX

Perseverance

> *Now for this very reason also, applying all diligence, in your faith supply moral excellence, and in your moral excellence, knowledge, and in your knowledge, self-control,* **and in your self-control, perseverance***, and in your perseverance, godliness, and in your godliness, brotherly kindness, and in your brotherly kindness, love.* — **2 Peter 1:5–7**

The word "perseverance" has a lot going on beneath the surface. The original Greek word is *hupomone*, with *hupo* meaning "under," and *meno* meaning "to stay, remain, or to abide." Thus, the word 'perseverance' literally means "to abide under."

The root idea of *hupomone* is to remain under some discipline—typically the subjecting of one's self to something he or she would normally and naturally rebel against. *Hupomone* means to steadfastly and unflinchingly bear up under a heavy load, in character (virtue), when under trial. It is forward looking, is spite of current circumstances. Theologian Leon Morris says *hupomone* carries with it the attitude of a soldier who in the thick of battle is not dismayed but fights on stoutly whatever the difficulties.[38]

Thus, biblical perseverance is not a "grin and bear it" kind of abiding, but the kind of abiding that faces whatever trial, affliction or difficult circumstance knowing that God is in control and purposes good in it.

It is interesting that Paul lists this word after self-control—which deals with handling the pleasures of life. Perseverance, on the other hand, deals with the problems of life. It is also closely related to the concept of hope. Notice that Paul writes in Romans 8:25 that "if we hope for what we do not see, with perseverance we wait eagerly for it" (NASB). Those who are confident in Christ and the promises of God in His Word know that deliverance from current circumstances—as well as the presence of sin—will come. This mindset of hope gives the believer Spirit-infused inner strength to "bear up" under anything.

Running the Whole Race—with Help

Back in 1992, a young man from England, Derek Redmond, participated in the Summer Olympic Games that were held in Barcelona, Spain. Derek was a runner competing in the 400-meter race. He had trained hard and prepared for many years to compete in the Olympics. However, during the final lap, he pulled a hamstring and fell over, writhing in pain. Derek was determined to finish; he stood up and limped toward the finish line. His father, watching from the stands, leaped over the retaining wall onto the track.

Jim Redmond, Derek's father, supported his son, who leaned on his shoulder the rest of the race. The crowd cheered as the two crossed the finish line--and when Derek finished, it was as if Derek, his father, and the onlookers had finished the race.

This is the call of Christians living out their faith in a fallen, sin-ridden world. Over and over in Scripture, Paul likens this journey to a race—and not an easy one to win! There will be "pulled hamstrings" along the way—persecution, trials, and afflictions. But the Word encourages believers to run and endure to the end, following the model of those who have gone before. And like Derek Redmond, Christians do not have to do it alone.

It will take all of your spiritual stamina to complete the journey, but Christ Himself will help carry you toward the finish line. When Jesus was about to ascend to the Father, He commissioned His disciples with the daunting and impossible task of taking the good news of His life, death and resurrection to the entire world! The disciples were likely in a state of shock—how would they ever complete such a task? And yet, Jesus immediately affirmed that they would have help along the way:

> And I will ask the Father, and he will give you another advocate to help you and be with you forever... — **John 14:16 (NIV)**

When Jesus left their presence, He did indeed send a helper and a comforter—the Holy Spirit—on the day of Pentecost. Those disciples, filled with the power of the

Holy Spirit, were enabled to spread the good news of the gospel to Jerusalem and Judea, and eventually through others who came after them, to ends of the Earth. Before leaving them, Jesus also said to His disciples, "And behold, I am with you always, to the end of the age" (Matthew 28:20 ESV). Jesus' words are a promise for the Christian today, too. Jesus is always present and will always help.

Hebrews states that we believers have a "great a cloud of witnesses surrounding us." These are those who have already run the race and are now with Jesus in heaven. The writer of Hebrews continues, "Let us also lay aside every weight, and the sin which so easily ensnares us, and let us run with endurance (*hupomone*) the race that is set before us, looking unto Jesus…" (Hebrews 12:1–2 NKJV).

Knowing this, and trusting God for His promise to help us on the journey, hope should replace any anxiety or fear when trials loom. It is like a person walking in a dark forest with no light except the occasional moonlight that breaks through the trees, momentarily lighting the path. Though that person may have to take ten steps in the dark before the path is lit again, that brief glimpse of solid ground illuminated by the moon provides hope for the person to keep walking, even when they can't see.

There Is a Prize for Persevering

Though the journey might be tough, not only is there hope for the future but there is blessing promised to the believer. God allows sufferings in people's lives to help them grow up and mature in Christ, but one day, believers who stand firm under rough circumstances in His name will receive what James refers to as "the crown of life."

> Blessed is the man who perseveres [hupomone] under trial, for once he has been approved, he will receive the crown of life which the Lord has promised to those who love him. — **James 1:12 (NASB)**

This "crown" refers to a wreath made of foliage or designed to resemble foliage worn by someone in biblical times of high status or held in high regard. It was an adornment worn around a person's head, crowning them victorious--typical in athletic games of the time. In those days, it showed appreciation for the victor's exceptional contribution to the state he represented. Paul used this same imagery in another verse:

> Do you not know that those who run in a race all run, but only one receives the prize? Run in such a way that you may win. Everyone who competes in the games exercises self-control in all things. They then do it to receive a perishable wreath, but we an imperishable. — **1 Corinthians 9:24-25 (NASB)**

Notice the imagery in both passages of Scripture; both allude to successfully completing a race and receiving a prize. However, for the believer, this "prize" is not a wreath that is perishable, but the reward for victory in Christ is eternal life with God. This triumphant life is available to God's children in the present and the eternal future.

How to Be Ready When Trials Come

Hard times will come. Trying circumstances will arise—guaranteed. Throwing in the towel as a believer may seem like the only option. Trials and afflictions should not come to the Christian as a surprise, however! The Bible prepared Christians for this—many times! God knew how hard it would be to stand firm, and in His love and grace, He let those who love Him know ahead of time.

How then should the believer prepare for potential periods of trial, or even suffering? We persevere.

Understand Why God Allows Suffering

The best thing a follower of Jesus can do to prepare for afflictions is to develop what John Piper calls a "theology of suffering"—to understand from a biblical perspective why suffering exists—and to solidify this foundation before trials hit. Understanding suffering means more than agreeing that yes, trials will come. It is much deeper. It means knowing who God is—His sovereignty, how He knows all things, how He is all powerful, and how everything He does and allows is on the basis of His great love for those He created.

Let's start by examining a few of Jesus' words on suffering:

> *Now there were some present at that time who told Jesus about the Galileans whose blood Pilate had mixed with their*

> sacrifices. Jesus answered, "Do you think that these Galileans were worse sinners than all the other Galileans because they suffered this way? I tell you, no! But unless you repent, you too will all perish." — ***Luke 13:1–3 (NIV)***

> Or those eighteen who died when the tower in Siloam fell on them—do you think they were more guilty than all the others living in Jerusalem? I tell you, no! But unless you repent, you too will all perish. — ***Luke 13:4–5 (NIV)***

Reflecting on the above verses, Don Carson writes: "What Jesus seems to presuppose is that all the sufferings of the world—whether caused by malice [as in Luke 13:1–3] or by accident [as in Luke 13:4–5]—are not peculiar examples of judgment falling on the distinctively evil, but rather examples of the bare, stark fact that we are all under sentence of death."[39]

Suffering is the reality of the fallen world—a world where sin separates people from their Creator. Without Christ, humanity stands under God's judgment. Though the believer is free from this bondage to sin, they still have to exist in a world that remains in that fallen state.

The hope for the believer is that God will one day reorder creation to where it was meant to be and will restore it and remove the effects of sin. One day, in Christ, everything will be made new. Until this happens, however, the world will continue to function dysfunctionally. Wars will spark; disease will spread, people will hate, and children will die. The only thing humanity can do is cry out like Job, "Though he slay me, yet will I trust him" (Job 13:15 KJV).

This is a short theology of suffering. It exists, and it will continue to exist until the Lord returns. Understanding this, believers can brace for trials before they occur so when they do, their faith will not only remain, but will be strengthened and, as James says below, "lacking in nothing":

> Count it all joy, my brothers, when you meet trials of various kinds, for you know that the testing of your faith produces steadfastness [hypomonē]. And let steadfastness [hypomonē] have its full effect, that you may be perfect and complete, lacking in nothing. — **James 1:2–4 (ESV)**

It will be impossible to fully understanding suffering from God's perspective without studying what the Bible has to say about it. Know that God hates when His children suffer and that He will be quick to comfort them:

> Praise be to the God and Father of our Lord Jesus Christ, the Father of compassion and the God of all comfort, who comforts us in all our troubles, so that we can comfort those in any trouble with the comfort we ourselves receive from God. — **2 Corinthians 1:3–4 (NIV)**

God also promises to restore those who have suffered:

> And the God of all grace, who called you to his eternal glory in Christ, after you have suffered a little while, will himself restore you and make you strong, firm and steadfast [hypomonē]. — **1 Peter 5:10 (NIV)**

Earthly suffering is temporary and we must persevere through it. God will deliver His people out of suffering, and what is ahead is far more wonderful than can be imagined!

The righteous person may have many troubles, but the LORD delivers him from them all... — **Psalm 34:19 (NIV)**

For our light and momentary troubles are achieving for us an eternal glory that far outweighs them all. — **2 Corinthians 4:17 (NIV)**

Who shall separate us from the love of Christ? Shall trouble or hardship or persecution or famine or nakedness or danger or sword? — **Romans 8:35 (NIV)**

I consider that our present sufferings are not worth comparing with the glory that will be revealed in us. — **Romans 8:18 (NIV)**

Nothing will separate God from those who love Him. The absolute worst that could happen to a person is nothing compared to the incomparable love of Christ. Again, this is the hope that will help the believer to be able to stand firm and persevere when trials hit!

Amy Carmichael writes in *Candles in the Dark*, "The best training is to learn to accept everything as it comes, as from Him whom our soul loves. The tests are always unexpected things, not great things that can be written up, but the common little rubs of life, silly little nothings, things you are ashamed of minding (at all). Yet they can knock a strong man over and lay him very low."[40]

When trials come, even the big ones will seem small for those who trust in Christ, are armed with the Word of God and have a proper understanding of why suffering exists. These are those who will never be knocked over!

What to Do When You Fail

> We are able to persevere only because God works within us, within our free wills. And because God is at work in us, we are certain to persevere. The decrees of God concerning election are immutable. They do not change, because He does not change. All whom He justifies He glorifies. None of the elect has ever been lost. — **R.C. Sproul**[41]

Though God desires that believers continue to stand firm and grow in their understanding of and obedience to Him, there will be times of failure. However, it does not have to be a way of life. The writer of Hebrews said, "Consider him [Jesus] who endured such opposition from sinners, so that you will not grow weary and lose heart. In your struggle against sin, you have not yet resisted to the point of shedding your blood" (Hebrews 12:3-4).

Love God through the temptation and do not lose heart or give up for "blowing it" too many times. Believe that overcoming the sin or the temptation of sin is possible, because it is. And then step out in faith to face another day in the power of the Holy Spirit. The Christian's battle is not a try-fail-try-fail struggle; rather, it is like Paul describes:

> We do not want you to be uninformed, brothers and sisters, about the troubles we experienced in the province of Asia. We were under great pressure, far beyond our ability to endure, so that we despaired of life itself. Indeed, we felt we had received the sentence of death. But this happened that we might not rely on ourselves but on God, who raises the dead. He has delivered us from such a deadly peril, and he will deliver us again. On him we have set our hope that he will continue to deliver us... — **2 Corinthians 1:8–10 (NIV)**

Paul acknowledged that the troubles he and his disciples went through were more than they could handle on their own. But notice Paul also saw the why of the troubles: so that they would not rely on themselves but on God!

God will deliver. Rather than sinking low because of unfortunate circumstances, difficult seasons, or a slide back to sin, turn to Him for comfort, peace, or forgiveness. Ask Him to work it out for your good and then don't look back but only ahead. Focus on the "crown of life" prepared for those who love Jesus! Run your race so that you will win! Press on and persevere!

WORKBOOK

Chapter 6 Questions

Question: Are you running the race—living life—to win the prize? How can you better allow God to help you finish strong?

_____
_____
_____
_____
_____
_____
_____
_____
_____
_____

Question: Why does God allow suffering?

_____
_____
_____
_____

_____
_____
_____
_____
_____
_____
_____

Question: How do you typically handle trials and failure? How can you let God help you through these times?

_____
_____
_____
_____
_____
_____
_____
_____

Action: Prepare yourself to run the race of your spiritual life all the way to the finish line, but at this same time, be willing to accept help—you need God's help! Know that there is blessing awaiting you at the end. Meanwhile, be ready when trials come by understanding why God allows suffering, studying God's Word, and knowing what to do when you fail. Trust God to deliver you through difficulties, love Him through times of temptation, and don't ever lose heart in doing what is right.

Chapter 6 Notes

CHAPTER SEVEN

Godliness

Now for this very reason also, applying all diligence, in your faith supply moral excellence, and in your moral excellence, knowledge, and in your knowledge, self-control, and in your self-control, perseverance, **and in your perseverance, godliness***, and in your godliness, brotherly kindness, and in your brotherly kindness, love.* — **2 Peter 1:5–7 (NASB)**

After challenging his readers to persevere—to endure trials of all kinds by focusing on what is ahead—Peter next calls disciples of Christ to persevere a certain kind of way: in faith, while striving to be godly.

"Godliness" is a term that might sound lofty or even esoteric. How can one be godly if there is only one God? Biblical godliness is a unique character quality. It is the inner reverent response that only those who believe in Jesus can exhibit to the things of God. The word "godliness" is from the Greek word *eusebeia*, with *eú* meaning "well" and *sébomai* meaning "to worship, to venerate, or to pay homage." So, 'godliness' means "well worship."

Paul explains godliness, or "well worship," in no uncertain terms in Romans:

> Therefore I urge you, brethren, by the mercies of God, to present your bodies a living and holy sacrifice, acceptable to God, which is your spiritual service of worship.— **Romans 12:1 (NASB)**

Worship is not a feeling a person gets when they sing a moving song or hymn in church; it is not a matter of raising hands or bowing heads. Worship is a verb, a response to God's presence and work in a person's life. This is what Paul meant when he says believers should present themselves as sacrifices to God—calling this act "worship."

Godliness is thus two parts. It is first (what's 2nd?) the attitude of the believer, living with a sense of God's presence. Godliness reflects a deep motivation instilled by the Holy Spirit to be led by love and the desire to please God. This attitude is then reflected in how a person lives before others and is especially evident toward those who are lost. This is the "doing what is pleasing to God," the second (?) aspect of godliness. It is the duty of the believer, what they will naturally be moved to do for God because of what God has done for them.

What Does Godliness Look Like?

When a person is godly, offering themselves as living sacrifices, what exactly does it look like?

A Godly Person is Obedient

In the New Testament, there is a Gentile man named Cornelius. The book of Acts describes him as a distinguished centurion at Caesarea in the Italian Regiment. Caesarea is a town halfway between modern-day Tel Aviv and Haifa, Israel. Peter writes that Cornelius "and all his family were devout and God-fearing..." (Acts 10:1-2 NIV). Later in Acts 10:22, some Jewish men told Peter that Cornelius was "a righteous and God-fearing man, who is respected by all the Jewish people" (NIV)). Cornelius prayed constantly and was generous to the poor.

When God instructed this Gentile officer to gather people to hear Peter's words, Cornelius obeyed. The word 'devout' in Acts 10:22 is the same word used to translate "godliness" in 1 Peter 2:6. The writer of Acts described Cornelius as one who worshiped God well. Godliness reacts to whatever God says in obedience. He acknowledged God's sovereignty,

A Godly Person Worships in Spirit and Truth

When Jesus was deep in conversation with the woman at the well in Samaria (John 4:6-30), He told her that "God is spirit, and his worshipers must worship in the Spirit and in truth" (John 4:24 NIV). This explains how a person should revere God—with praise and adoration of the Creator of all things—and should worship God with one's whole heart. Moses describes worshiping in the Spirit, saying, "You shall love the LORD your God with all your heart and with all your soul and with all your might" (Deuteronomy 6:5 ESV). Worshiping in the Spirit is the overflow from the heart of a person's love and reverence for God.

In Hebrews, this heart overflow is called "the fruit of lips that openly profess his name" (Hebrews 13:15 NIV). Hosea calls worship the same thing: "Take words with you and return to the LORD. Say to Him, 'Take away all iniquity and receive us graciously, that we may present the fruit of our lips'" (Hosea 14:2 NASB).

"Fruit" in these verses refers to what is produced by an organism—in this case the fruit produced by the one worshiping God. David Guzik, comments, "Because we do have an altar (the cross) and we do have a High Priest (Jesus), we should always offer sacrifices. But they are not the bloody sacrifices of the old covenant, but the sacrifice of praise, the fruit of our lips."[42] The overflow from the heart of the believer—the fruit of their lips— is praise.

To worship in truth, however, there must also be knowledge of the one receiving the worship. This "truth" is the increasing knowledge of Jesus that results in an emotional response to God that appropriately brings honor to His name. Without knowledge of the truth, worship will not be much more than an overly emotional experience. The godly person worships in Spirit and in truth.

A Godly Person Studies and Keeps the Word of God

Often Scripture reveals that a believer's response to God's Word is directly related to his or her relationship with Him. For example, Jesus said, "If you love Me, you will keep My commandments" (John. 14:15 NASB). Notice how loving God is reflected in two things: knowing and keeping His commandments. To know His commandments, one must read, study, and meditate on His divinely inspired Word. However, the second part of Jesus' instruction is to "keep" them. Typically, in the Christian world, the term used is "obey." However, let's consider what Jesus might actually be teaching.

The word "keep" is the Greek word *tēreō*, meaning "to attend to carefully, to take care of, or to guard."

In the Old Testament, in Deuteronomy, God says, "Love the LORD your God and always keep His charge, His statutes, His ordinances, and His commandments" (Deuteronomy 11:1 NASB). Here the English word "keep" in the original Hebrew is *shamar*. It, too, means "to guard or watch over."

There is so much depth to this command to keep God's commandments! Yes, there should be an active response to the commands in Scripture. If God says to flee from sexual immorality or other temptations, the believer should flee out of obedience. But *why*? Because Christians have been charged with the high call of guarding and carefully caring for and highly regarding God's instruction. They are called to protect it like a soldier, to guard it with their life. God says the person who does so exhibits godliness and ultimately it expresses love for Him.

> When we seek His word above all others, His encouragement before all others, His truth instead of all others, then we will be pleasing to Him more than all others. — **Woodrow Kroll**[43]

A Godly Person Reflects Christ

Thirdly, godliness can be seen in a person whose life exhibits Christ. Steve Diaz, says, "A godly person is one who acts properly, reacts properly, and leaves no doubt in anyone's mind that he/she is a child of God. God is seen in this person from the inside out and from the outside in."[44]

Once people put their faith in Jesus as Lord and Savior, they are new creations and Paul says they are "being renewed in knowledge after the image of [their] Creator" (Colossians 3:10 NIV). What was severed back in the garden—God's children walking in intimate relationship with Him and reflecting His character—is now renewed and continually being restored.

> And we all, with unveiled face, beholding the glory of the Lord, **are being transformed into the same image** from one degree of glory to another. For this comes from the Lord who is the Spirit. — **2 Corinthians 3:18 (ESV, emphasis added)**

As the believer adds to their faith goodness and knowledge of God, and exhibits self-control and perseverance through trials and tribulations, he should be reflecting Christ to a lost world. Reacting in a godly way will cause people to look and be drawn not to the person, but to God. Jesus said that through His death He would draw all men to himself (John 12:32). How? Jesus' death put an end to separation between man and God, for those who believe in Jesus:

> For whosoever shall call upon the name of the Lord shall be saved. How then shall they call on him in whom they have not believed? and how shall they believe in him of whom they have not heard? and how shall they hear without a preacher? — **Romans 10:13–14 (KJV)**

Those who believe in Jesus have the Spirit dwelling within them. As they keep God's instruction, they reflect His image to those around them and Scripture says God will then draw them to Himself. This is the victory the Christian is persevering for—to fight against the enemy who would like nothing more than for the believer to exhibit characteristics other than Christ such as fear, doubt, anger, evil and malice. However, those who reflect Jesus are a force to be reckoned with! Charles Spurgeon reflects on those who are godly, saying:

> Poor, sickly believers turn the church into a hospital, rather than an army. Oh, to have a church built up with the deep godliness of people who know the Lord in their very hearts, and will seek to follow the Lamb wherever he goes![45]

The Life of the Godly

Dr. Ralph F. Wilson writes, "Godliness is not a synonym for boring."[46] Jesus and the disciples were far from boring! Their lives were full of action and suspense. The dead were raised to life! Illnesses were healed! And hearts were supernaturally transformed! This, too, is the abundant life promised for all believers who desire godliness.

The godly person seeks to please God by submitting to Him and His authority in their lives, by walking in the gentle leading of the Holy Spirit dwelling within them. The godly person yields continually and humbly to God's desires, rather than his or her own.

Remember, however, that that this takes training. Paul wrote to "train yourself to be godly. For physical training is of some value, but godliness has value for all things, holding promise for both the present life and the life to come" (1 Timothy 4:7b–8 NIV).

To "train" is the Greek word *gymnazō*, where the English word 'gym' or 'gymnasium' comes from. It means to undergo some sort of discipline Training is to practice something to perfection. Gymnasts will practice hours and hours on one acrobatic move, developing it so that they might perform it within a routine flawlessly. Paul says physical training such as this has some value, but how much more valuable is spiritual training!

It will be work and will take commitment. But Paul says practicing godliness holds promise beyond this life. This is the hope of heaven for the believer!

WORKBOOK

Chapter 7 Questions

Question: Do you worship God in Spirit and in truth? How can you make sure you're seeking God on His terms?

_____
_____
_____
_____
_____
_____
_____
_____
_____
_____
_____

Question: Look over your life. In what specific ways have you grown in godliness by keeping God's Word continuously?

Question: How do you reflect Christ on a daily basis? How can you better reflect Christ?

Action: Worship well! Seek God on His terms, worshiping in Spirit and in truth. Study and keep the Word of God. Then reflect Christ in how you act and speak on a daily basis. Remember, pursuing godliness is far from boring—it's hard-core spiritual training!

Chapter 7 Notes

CHAPTER EIGHT

Brotherly Kindness

John the apostle spoke harshly against anyone who said they believed in Jesus and loved Him but could not love another person, or "brother.". :

> *Whoever claims to love God yet hates a brother or sister is a liar. For whoever does not love their brother and sister, whom they have seen, cannot love God, whom they have not seen. And he has given us this command: Anyone who loves God must also love their brother and sister.* — *1 John 4:20–21 (NIV)*

The first six virtues we have discussed so far in this book—diligence, faith, moral excellence, knowledge, self-control, perseverance, and godliness—concern a person's inner life and relationship with God. The last two we will study, brotherly kindness and love,, relate to a person's outward life. In fact, brotherly kindness is an outward expression of the inward transformation occurring from salvation. It should be the natural overflow of what is going on in a person's heart.

Brotherly kindness is passionate yet practical compassion for others and thus closely connected with godliness. This is why Peter lists them one after the other:

> *Now for this very reason also, applying all diligence, in your faith supply moral excellence, and in your moral excellence, knowledge, and in your knowledge, self-control, and in your self-control, perseverance, and in your perseverance, godliness, **and in your godliness, brotherly kindness,** and in your brotherly kindness, love.* — **2 Peter 1:5–7 (NASB, emphasis added)**

In God's economy, in Christ, slaves and free people were on level playing ground, each calling Jesus their Lord. Perhaps this is why Peter was insistent on teaching about this kind of brotherly love, knowing that such a diverse cultural community would need this emphasis on love of the brethren for it to survive! From this concept, Peter now calls Christians in their godliness, to exhibit brotherly kindness.

Another version translates the phrase "brotherly kindness" as "mutual affection" (NIV). There are three types of love in the Greek language, and each means something very different. One type, *eros love*, is more passion-focused while another type, *agape* love, is selfless, submissive love. We'll talk about those two more in chapter 9. But in 2 Peter 7, Peter is speaking of a third type of love: *phileo* love.

Brotherly love, or "mutual affection," is a unique expression of emotion. The concept is drawn from the Greek word *philadelphia* which comes originally from two words: *phílos*, which means, "beloved, dear, and friendly," and *adelphós*, meaning "brother." Thus, *philadelphia* means "fraternal love" or "brotherly love, or kindness." This is where the term '*phileo* love' comes from.

Phileo love is exhibited most obviously within a family: two children, as different as they could be experiencing a fraternal, kind love as brothers united under the same parents.

Who Are My Brothers?

In biblical times, brotherly love (*philadelphia*) normally referred to the love family members held for each other. However, in the New Testament, *philadelphia* is often the word writers chose to communicate the love believers possessed for one another though they were from different biological families, Christ connected them as family with God's love uniting them together. When people put their faith in Christ, they become part of God's family—and each woman or man who believes become like a brother or sister. The new believer belongs now to a new spiritual family.

The world was turned upside down because of Christianity. A radical relationship between Jews and Greeks— two people groups that hated each other— was birthed. In spite of people's diverse status and backgrounds, this affection for each other amazed the pagans who were looking in and wondering what was going on!

This sounds a bit like joining together was easy, but this new relationship with people one used to hate was sometimes difficult. And it will be for us, too. With brothers and sisters in Christ, we must be willing bear each other's burdens and forgive shortcomings and failures.

Paul, too, was passionate about love for the brethren. He used this word *philadelphia* nineteen times in 1 Thessalonians alone! Christians are not supposed to be casual friends with each other but to express a deep, bonding familial type of love. Check out other uses of *philadelphia* in the New Testament; clearly, the New Testament writers saw this new love for the brethren as paramount:

> *Be devoted to one another in love [philadelphia]. Honor one another above yourselves.* — **Romans 12:10 (NIV)**

> *Now about your love [philadelphia] for one another we do not need to write to you, for you yourselves have been taught by God to love [philadelphia] each other.* — **1 Thessalonians 4:9 (NIV)**

> *Let brotherly love [philadelphia] continue.* — **Hebrews 13:1 (KJV)**

> *Now that you have purified yourselves by obeying the truth so that you have sincere love [philadelphia] for each other, love [philadelphia] one another deeply, from the heart.* — **1 Peter 1:22 (NIV)**

Brotherly love is a love of belonging to something far beyond what is comprehendible. It is a love that exists between God's children and is what unites them with the Father. The natural expression of that love makes two people who might normally hate each other, family. What does this kind of affectionate love look like?

How to Show Brotherly Kindness

Encourage One Another

One of the best ways to extend this type of affection toward other believers is to encourage them. The writer of Hebrews exhorts Christians to spur one another on "toward love and good deeds, not giving up meeting together, as some are in the habit of doing, but encouraging one another—and all the more as you see the Day approaching" (Hebrews 1:24–25 NIV). As this world continues to grow more evil and dark, God instructs believers to hold each other up and come alongside each other. In fact, this is exactly what the word "encourage" means! In Greek, it is the word *parakaleo*, from *para*, meaning "side of" and *kaleo*, meaning "to call." Thus, to encourage means "to call one alongside." Kent Hughes, gives this illustration for encouraging one another: "I see this [*parakaleo*] exemplified every time my church has a roller skating party, and the parents put their little ones on skates for the first time. Mom and Dad skate with their child, holding on to his or her hands, sometimes with the child's feet on the ground and sometimes in the air. But all the time the parents are alongside encouraging the child."[47]

Brotherly love comes alongside other believers and "holds their hands" in a sense—encouraging them along in the journey toward the finish line in Christ, and hopefully helping them not fall!

Rejoice—and Weep—with Your Brothers

A friend of mine lost his father a few years ago. After the ceremony, he recalls turning around to see two of his closest friends walking up; moved to tears, my friend embraced them. No words were exchanged, but the understanding between, though unspoken, ran deep. These two friends were expressing brotherly love by coming alongside my friend in one of his darkest hours.

Romans 12:15 says, "Rejoice with those who rejoice, and weep with those who weep" (NASB). It's great to show up when things are good—to be part of someone's life during times of celebration. But God also calls Christians to demonstrate personal interest and care for others in the body of Christ when things aren't so good. Will we be like Christ, who when approaching Lazarus' grave, entered into Mary and Martha's sorrow? Scripture tells us "Jesus wept"—likely for more than the loss of Lazarus' life (John 11:35 NIV). He wept alongside his friends, who were experiencing deep pain.

However, Paul also says to "rejoice with those who rejoice." In this verse, the word "rejoice" is focusing on the redemptive work of God coming to fruition in the person of Jesus Christ. Therefore, we are to enjoy celebrating with others when God's goodness is evident in their life!

Abstain from Gossip

A person might be the most religious, committed, "holy" person walking around, but if they cannot control their tongue James says the are deceiving their own heart. Worse, James says this person's religion—or their worship of God—is thus "worthless" (James 1:26 NASB). It is in vanity and useless and has no real or lasting value.

How important is it then to control what comes out of our mouth? Unfortunately, what so easily spews out of many of our mouths in all its ugliness is gossip.

Gossip is one of the most potent issues even among fellow believers. In fact, Paul includes gossip in his list of pretty dark sins of those with a depraved mind: all unrighteousness, wickedness, greed, evil, envy, murder, strife, lies and malice, God-hating, arrogance, and boastfulness (Romans 1:29–30). The book of Proverbs warns, too, of the deadly allure of gossip and its lethal effects: "The words of a gossip are like choice morsels; they go down to the inmost parts" (Proverbs 26:22 NIV). Gossip has a corrupting effect; it sinks its sharp teeth down into people's hearts and corrodes their minds—spreading like cancer.

The New Testament word for "gossip" (*psithuristes*, Romans 1:29) in the original Greek is literally "a whisperer"—a person who murmurs behind another person's back with the intention of harming them. If believers are supposed to be extending brotherly love to each other, lifting each other up and walking alongside them on their journey, how can any form of gossip—whispering behind each other's back with intent to hurt—be anything but evil? There is no question-- gossip speaks death, but God calls Christians to choose life (Deuteronomy 30:19).

> A gossiper is someone who pours out his poison by whispering in our ears. — **Godet**[48]

May we never be that person who "pours out poison" by speaking falsely of our brothers and sisters in Christ—or anyone else for that matter!

Extend Forgiveness

Something happens in a person's soul when they choose not to forgive. Bitterness sinks in. They become hardened. And soon, they become bound to the issue they are not resolved to forgive, rather than experiencing freedom by letting go of a grievance. There is blessing for forgiving!

Even secular psychologists see the benefits from choosing to forgive, noting how forgiveness can contribute to healing from damage done by the offender. But more than that, it helps a person let go of anger, helps a person focus on the future rather than the past, and helps a person re-learn trust. Jesus taught, "Be merciful, just as your Father is merciful. Do not judge, and you will not be judged. Do not condemn, and you will not be condemned.

Forgive, and you will be forgiven" (Luke 6:36–37 NIV, emphasis added). Above all, because forgiveness is not something we can do on our own, it ensures God's presence is active in our lives. This is why Jesus died on the cross—so that our sins could be forgiven. If Jesus forgave us, when we were so undeserving, how much more should we forgive others?

C.S. Lewis writes, "To be a Christian means to forgive the inexcusable, because God has forgiven the inexcusable in you."[49] Forgiveness isn't something we grant because others deserve it; we extend it to others because God first forgave us (Ephesians 4:31–32).

Extend brotherly love to others by choosing to wipe the slate clean—give up the right to hurt others in exchange for being hurt. After all, "For if you forgive other people when they sin against you, your heavenly Father will also forgive you. But if you do not forgive others their sins, your Father will not forgive your sins" (Matthew 6:14-15 NIV).

Help to Restore Those in Sin

Sometimes, brotherly love involves restoring someone who has fallen into sin. God commands this pretty clearly in Galatians 6:1:

> Brothers and sisters, if someone is caught in a sin, you who live by the Spirit should restore that person gently. But watch yourselves, or you may also be tempted. — **Galatians 6:1 (NIV)**

When someone who professes to be a believer falls in to sin, perhaps not deliberately even, Paul says restoration is the ultimate goal. Restore is a verb that commands instruction for the Christian. "Restore" means to put something back to its former condition. It was a medical term in the Greek culture of the day, referring to re-setting a broken bone. If a broken bone is left un-set, it can result in nerve damage and even permanent loss of feeling. It can grow back incorrectly and might affect mobility.

In the same way, if a Christian who has fallen into some sin is not gently re-directed back to restoration, the results may be long-lasting. Damage may occur—not just to the person who sinned, but to others caught in the wake of sin's destructive path.

Sometimes restoration is not easy, and sometimes it's not even welcomed by the believer. However, Christians are still called to participate in it.

Along with showing these types of brotherly kindness, God asks us to also show a deep love for one another. But this second type of love is distinct from what we've been talking about in this chapter—it runs even deeper.

WORKBOOK

Chapter 8 Questions

Question: Which "brothers" or groups of people do you need to work on loving as family?

_____
_____
_____
_____
_____
_____
_____
_____
_____
_____
_____

Question: Which of your brothers in Christ do you need to encourage today? How, specifically, can you encourage them?

Question: Which of your brothers in Christ needs to be restored? How can you help to heal and restore them today?

Action: Be kind! Love others, especially fellow believers, as intensely and completely as you might love a blood relative. This holds true even if you come from different backgrounds! Know who your brothers in Christ are, and show them brotherly love by encouraging them, rejoicing and weeping with them, abstaining from gossip about them, forgiving them, and helping to heal and restore them when they stumble spiritually.

Chapter 8 Notes

CHAPTER NINE

Love—with Sacrifice

The love Christians have for other brothers and sisters in Christ is like the love between family members—a warm, familiar, friendship kind of love similar to what might exist between siblings. It is the love of belonging, based on likeness. But Peter immediately connects this type of love with a much deeper love: *agape*.

> *Now for this very reason also, applying all diligence, in your faith supply moral excellence, and in your moral excellence, knowledge, and in your knowledge, self-control, and in your self-control, perseverance, and in your perseverance, godliness, and in your godliness, brotherly kindness, and in your brotherly kindness,* **love**. *— 2 Peter 1:5–7 (NASB)*

Kenneth Wuest, says that *phileo* love is a friendly love, called out of one's heart as a response to the pleasure one took in a person or object and based upon an inner community between the person loving and the person or object loved.[50] It is a love, based on emotion, that we discussed in depth in previous chapter. This next kind of love, however, is a love of devotion.

Do you see the difference? Let's look deeper.

This love, called *agape* in Greek, is sacrificial love. It biblically refers to a love that originates in God—that He reflects and enables in His children. *Agape* love is a love that denies the self for the benefit of the object loved. John MacArthur says that Christians have no capacity to generate this kind of *agape* love on our own. It's a sacrificial love we can't generate but we can generate it by being humble/obedient....). He further explains, "The Greek word for that kind of love ... is characterized by humility, obedience to God, and self-sacrifice."[51]

According to James Packer in his book *Your Father Loves You*, *agape* is "virtually a Christian invention—a new word for a new thing (apart from about twenty occurrences in the Greek version of the Old Testament, it is almost non-existent before the New Testament)." Packer writes that *agape* draws its meaning directly from the revelation of God in Christ. It is not a form of natural affection, but a supernatural fruit of the Spirit (Galatians 5:22). It is a matter of will rather than feeling (for Christians must love even those they dislike, as taught in Matthew 5:44–48).[52]

Agape love is the most tangible expression of God, and the basic element of what makes one like Christ. When agape love is expressed, others looking in see none other than the Spirit of the living God flowing out from the person. *Agape* love is not passionate love—coming and going like the wind, focused on internal desires. It is also not something that can be acquired by work or exercise or even discipline. It is unconditional, and it is selfless.

God's Kind of Love

The Bible reveals that that God is love (*agape*) in 1 John 4:8, and that He loved the world so much that He gave His only son Jesus that whoever would believe in Him would have life everlasting (John 3:16). This love went to the cross for you, and for me. This love saw all of my sin and all of your sin and forgave anyway. And in spite of that sin, this love made a way to mend the broken relationship between God and His people—at a high cost. This is humble, sacrificial, and unconditional *agape* love.

The Bible teaches what this love looks like most clearly in 1 Corinthians 13:4–8. I'm sure you've heard it before—it's the common passage of Scripture quoted at weddings. But read it closely, and consider God's *agape* love in light of what you've learned about the spiritual qualities that make for a mature, Spirit-filled and fruit-bearing Christian. Consider the power when God's agape love aligns with diligence, moral excellence knowledge, self-control, perseverance, godliness, and kindness. *Agape* love is intertwined with all of these virtues! It inspires and empowers them!

> *Love is patient, love is kind and it is not jealous; love does not brag and is not arrogant, does not act unbecomingly; it does not seek its own, is not provoked, does not take into account a wrong suffered, does not rejoice in unrighteousness, but rejoices with the truth; bears all things, believes all things, hopes all things, endures all things. Love never fails...*
> *— 1 Corinthians 13:4–8 (NASB)*

It is this kind of patient, kind, humble, selfless love that changes the world. This is *godly* love.

Loving the Lost

The Bible says that there are two purposes for the believer: to Love God and to love others. This comes directly from Matthew 22:37. The whole Bible is summed up in knowing God and then sharing God's love with others. This is the called the gospel—the good news of Jesus Christ.

Agape love looks outward, to a lost world that is not only far from this kind of love but eternally separated from the One who is agape love. Agape love inspires us to love the lost, for this is the heart of God:

> For the Son of Man came to seek and to save the lost. —
> **Luke 19:10 (NIV)**

Jesus humbled Himself and became obedient to the worst kind of death imaginable at that time—death by crucifixion—, expressing agape love in absolute fullness. Why? To save the lost. And He would have done it if you or I were the only person on earth who needed saving. In Luke 15:4 Jesus taught His disciples, "Suppose one of you has a hundred sheep and loses one of them. Doesn't he leave the ninety-nine in the open country and go after the lost sheep until he finds it?" (NIV). Because of love, He seeks His lost sheep and gave His life that they would follow Him.

Love Like Jesus

> I pray that you will understand the words of Jesus, "Love one another as I have loved you." Ask yourself, "How has he loved me? Do I really love others in the same way?" Unless this love is among us, we can kill ourselves with work and it will only be work, not love. Work without love is slavery. — **Mother Teresa**[53]

As Jesus gently comes alongside us, loves us with agape love, so too are we to do the same for others. This is the call of the follower of Christ: to love others as Christ has loved us.

Loving others is the basis of our call to evangelism and discipleship. It is not a call to work for the sake of Christian work, but a response to this crazy, mind-blowing, deeply personal and always unconditional love of God. It is sharing this love with others and teaching them to do the same.

One of the most impactful women in our world was Mother Teresa. She spent her entire life helping the poorest of the poor in India. She described the purpose of her charity, the Missionaries of Charity, as taking care of the hungry, the naked, the homeless, the crippled, the blind, the lepers—all those people who feel unwanted, unloved, uncared for throughout society.

Sounds a lot like Jesus, doesn't it?

This is God's love! God's love knows no boundaries, ethnic barriers, social class divisions or monetary status. No, it cares for all people and it is this sacrificial love that will bring salvation to the world. Perhaps Tertullian said it best: "It is our care for the helpless, our practice of loving-kindness, that brands us in the eyes of many of our opponents. 'Look!' they say, 'How they love one another! Look how they are prepared to die for one another.'"

This is what unconditional, *agape*, 1 Corinthians 13 love looks like. This is the character of God

WORKBOOK

Chapter 9 Questions

Question: What's the difference between brotherly and *agape* love? What does God's love mean to you?

_____
_____
_____
_____
_____
_____
_____
_____
_____
_____
_____

Question: When have you showed *agape* love to others? When has someone else showed *agape* love to you?

_____
_____

Question: To whom do you need to share the gospel—even at your own risk or inconvenience? What's the first step you will take?

Action: Develop *agape* love for others—God's kind of love, more than just the attachment and devotion amongst family members. *Agape* love means you must love others even when it hurts; it is a sacrificial love. Therefore, love the lost too, enough to share the gospel with them even when it's inconvenient, difficult, scary, or dangerous to do so. We are called to love everyone, like Jesus did!

Chapter 9 Notes

CONCLUSION

Why a Godly Life?

Peter writes to the early believers, and thus also to us, about the inherent qualities in a follower of Christ who is maturing. Some of the qualities might not be as developed as others, but all should be progressing forward. Quoting Stephen Paine, Peter's presentation of these characteristics seems to "observe an order from the more elemental to the more advanced, but they are all facets of the Spirit's work in the life of a believer, aspects of the glory of the indwelling Christ, His character shown in the Christian's character."[54]

In this book we've focused on 2 Peter 1:5–7. Let's read it one more time:

> *Now for this very reason also, applying all diligence, in your faith supply moral excellence, and in your moral excellence, knowledge, and in your knowledge, self-control, and in your self-control, perseverance, and in your perseverance, godliness, and in your godliness, brotherly kindness, and in your brotherly kindness, love.* **— 2 Peter 1:5-7 (NASB)**

However, we must not miss the rest of the passage, verses 8–12. This is the "why" of possessing these qualities, the whole reason for pursuing these things in the first place!

> *If these qualities are yours and are increasing, they render you neither useless nor unfruitful in the true knowledge of our Lord Jesus Christ. For he who lacks these qualities is blind or short-sighted, having forgotten his purification from his former sins. Therefore, brethren, be all the more diligent to make certain about His calling and choosing you; for as long as you practice these things, you will never stumble; for in this way the entrance into the eternal kingdom of our Lord and Savior Jesus Christ will be abundantly supplied to you. Therefore, I will always be ready to remind you of these things, even though you already know them, and have been established in the truth which is present with you.* — *2 Peter 1:8-12*

When believers diligently and in faith supply moral excellence, knowledge, self-control, and when they persevere in godliness, brotherly kindness, and ultimately love, the Bible says they will never be useless! Rather than being "blind" or "short-sighted," they will be fruitful in the true knowledge of Christ. Most importantly, Peter says, "for as long as you practice these things, you will never stumble," and the entrance to the eternal kingdom of God will be supplied—in abundance. What blessing!

Growing in faith is a journey. It is not a one-time deal, and it is not a check-off list. It is a life lived in close step with the Spirit of God, who walks alongside us the entire way. As Peter shows, faith is the foundation for the believer, and unconditional agape love, listed last, is the climax. For the Christian, this means cooperating with God in producing a Christian life which is a credit to Him.[2]

These virtues in increasing measure will result in spiritual fruit that reflects God's great love for us. This is the life we are in pursuit of—this is the godly life!

---

[2] Michael Green, *The Second Epistle General of Peter and the General Epistle of Jude*, p. 67.

REFERENCES

Notes

1. Ivy, Dan.
2. Gallup, George, and Jim Castelli.
3. Barna Group. www.barna.org.
4. Gray, James M. "How to Eat the Word." *Positive Words with Peter Wade*. Positive Word Ministries. http://peterwade.com/articles/other/eatword.shtml
5. Butcher, Carmen Acevedo. "Cows and Scripture." *The Well Blog*. Intervarsity Christian Fellowship/USA. 26 April 2013. http://thewell.intervarsity.org/blog/cows-and-scripture
6. Warren, Rick *Rick Warren's Bible Study Methods: Twelve Ways You Can Unlock God's Word*. Zondervan, 2006.
7. Lewis, C. S. *Mere Christianity*. 1952.
8. *Our Daily Bread*.
9. "Religion in the News." *Sign of the Times*. March 1997.

10. "Faith." *Merriam-Webster Learner's Dictionary.* http://www.merriam-webster.com/dictionary/faith
11. Tozer, A. W. In "A. W. Tozer > Quotes > Quotable Quote." *Goodreads.com.* Goodreads. Inc. http://www.goodreads.com/quotes/349634-we-can-be-in-our-day-what-the-heroes-of
12. Spurgeon, Charles. In "19 Amazing Quotes about Living by Faith." *Christian Quotes.* Telling Ministries LLC. http://www.christianquotes.info/top-quotes/19-amazing-quotes-about-living-by-faith/
13. Tozer, A. W. In "The Pursuit of God Quotes." *Goodreads.com.* Goodreads. Inc. https://www.goodreads.com/work/quotes/203894-pursuit-of-god
14. Spurgeon, Charles. In "Beliefnet's Inspirational Quotes." *Beliefnet.* Beliefnet, Inc. http://www.beliefnet.com/quotes/evangelical/c/c-h-spurgeon/if-we-cannot-believe-god-when-circumstances-seem-b.aspx
15. Mounce, William D. *Complete Expository Dictionary of Old & New Testament Words.* Grand Rapids: Zondervan, 2006, p. 593.
16. Tozer, A. W. In "20 Christian Quotes by A. W. Tozer." *Christian Quotes.* Telling Ministries LLC. http://www.christianquotes.info/top-quotes/20-christian-quotes-by-a-w-tozer/
17. Chan, Francis.
18. Snyder, Michael.

19. MacArthur, John F. *Can God Bless America?* Thomas Nelson, 2002.
20. "Moral." *Merriam-Webster's Dictionary.*
21. Chesterton, G. K.
22. De Haan, Mart.
23. Walvoord, John F., and Roy B. Zuck. *Bible Knowledge Commentary* (New ed.). David C. Cook, 2002.
24. Spurgeon, Charles. In "Spurgeon's Verse Expositions of the Bible: 2 Peter 1." *StudyLight.org.* StudyLight.org. https://www.studylight.org/commentaries/spe/2-peter-1.html
25. King, Guy H. "His Courteous Address, Colossians 1:3–11." *Crossing the Border: An Expositional Study of Colossians.* 1957. From *Baptist Bible Believer's Website.* http://www.baptistbiblebelievers.com/NTStudies/EpistleofPaultotheColossiansbyGuyKing/tabid/193/Default.aspx
26. Haak, Carl.
27. Brother Lawrence. *The Practice of the Presence of God.*
28. Bridges, Jerry.
29. Thomas, Gary. *The Glorious Pursuit: Embracing the Virtues of Christ.* NavPress, 1998.
30. Krejcir, Richard.
31. Piper, John. "The Fierce Fruit of Self-Control." *Bethlehem Baptist Church.* Bethlehem Baptist Church. 15 May 2001.

http://www.hopeingod.org/document/fierce-fruit-self-control
32. Author unknown. *Record of Christian Work.*
33. Sproul, R. C. In "24 R. C. Sproul Quotes." *Christian Quotes.* Telling Ministries LLC. http://www.christianquotes.info/quotes-by-author/r-c-sproul-quotes/
34. Nee, Watchman. "The Normalcy of the Spirit." *The Spiritual Man.* http://www3.telus.net/trbrooks/normalcyspirit.htm
35. Crockett, Kent. *The 911 Handbook.* Peabody, MA.: Hendrickson, 2003, p. 35.
36. LeClaire, Jennifer. "You're Resisting the Devil, So Why Won't He Flee?" *Charisma News.* Charisma Media. 5 October 2013. http://www.charismanews.com/opinion/41239-you-re-resisting-the-devil-so-why-won-t-he-flee
37. Dryden, John. In "John Dyden > Quotes > Quotable Quote." *Goodreads.com.* Goodreads. Inc. http://www.goodreads.com/quotes/83576-better-shun-the-bait-than-struggle-in-the-snare
38. Morris, Leon.
39. Carson, Don.
40. Carmichael, Amy. *Candles in the Dark.* Christian Literature Crusade, 1982.
41. Sproul, R. C. In "R. C. Sproul Quote — God at Work in Us." *Christian Quotes.* Telling Ministries LLC.
http://www.christianquotes.info/images/r-c-sproul-quote-god-work-us/

42. Guzik, David. "Hebrews 13—Living a Positive Christian Life." *Enduring Word.* https://enduringword.com/commentary/hebrews-13/
43. Kroll, Woodrow. In "39 Quotes about Godliness." *Christian Quotes.* Telling Ministries LLC. http://www.christianquotes.info/quotes-by-topic/quotes-about-godliness/
44. Diaz, Steve.
45. Spurgeon, Charles. In David Guzik, "1 Kings 5—Preparations to Build the Temple." *Enduring Word.* https://enduringword.com/commentary/1-kings-5/
46. Ralph F. Wilson. "Godliness—a Forgotten Christian Virtue." *Jesus Walk Bible Study Series.* http://www.jesuswalk.com/timothy/godliness.htm
47. Hughes, Kent. In "Hebrews 13:22–25 Commentary." *Precept Austin.* http://preceptaustin.org/hebrews_1322-25.htm
48. Godet. In Charles Kimball, "Gossip: The 8th Deadly Sin Proverbs 18:8." *Preaching.com.* 1 March 2002. http://www.preaching.com/sermons/11565825/
49. Lewis, C. S. In "C. S. Lewis > Quotes > Quotable Quote." *Goodreads.com.* Goodreads. Inc. http://www.goodreads.com/quotes/103229-to-be-a-christian-means-to-forgive-the-inexcusable-because
50. Wuest, Kenneth.

51. MacArthur, John. *Drawing Near.* Crossway, 2002.
52. Packer, James. *Your Father Loves You: Daily Insights for Knowing God.* Harold Shaw, 1986.
53. Mother Teresa. In "Mother Teresa > Quotes > Quotable Quote." *Goodreads.com.* Goodreads. Inc. http://www.goodreads.com/quotes/74313-i-pray-that-you-will-understand-the-words-of-jesus
54. Paine, Stephen W. "The Second Epistle of Peter." In *The Wycliffe Bible Commentary*, p. 1458.

About the Author

Jody Burkeen is the founder and president of MAN UP! Gods Way Ministries and the pastor of Ignite Church in Eureka, MO. Man Up God's Way ministry was birthed out of a desire to change the way Christian men "do" Christianity.

Jody's self-described "Damascus Road Transformation" led him on a journey to search the Scripture to find what he had been missing his whole life, which was Jesus Christ. In this journey, the Word of God took over in a way he never expected. Searching for men in the church to help him in his walk, he found very little help. What he did find was men that needed the same kind of help he did.

Through MAN UP! Gods Way Ministry it is Jody's hope that he can challenge men to live a separated life on fire for God.

He is the author of the Amazon Best Seller Man Up- Becoming a Godly Man in an Ungodly World. He is also a co-Author for The Marriage Advance.

Jody is married to his wife of 27 years, Nan. They have 4 children 16,15, and twins 6-years-old.

About Sermon To Book

SermonToBook.com began with a simple belief that sermons should be touching lives, not collecting dust. That's why we turn sermons into high-quality books that are accessible to people all over the globe.

Turning your sermon series into a book exposes more people to God's Word, better equips you for counseling, accelerates future sermon preparation, adds credibility to your ministry, and even helps make ends meet during tight financial times.

John 21:25 tells us that the world itself couldn't contain the books that would be written about the work of Jesus Christ. Our mission is to try anyway. Because, in Heaven, there will no longer be a need for sermons or books. Our time is now.

If God so leads you, we'd love to work with you on your sermon or sermon series.

Visit www.sermontobook.com to learn more.